Twenty Centuries of Jewish Life in the Holy Land

The Forgotten Generations

Editor: Dan Bahat

PREFACE

The Land of Israel, once called Canaan and much later Palestine, is indissolubly bound up with the Jewish people. Here Jewish history began four thousand years ago. Throughout those centuries there have always been Jews in the Land. In exile and in dispersion the Jews cherished it in their hearts and repeatedly sought to return. Although the Land was occupied by alien conquerors, no other people ever attained independence here or regarded it as the core and centre of national existence.

During almost half of the biblical period the Land was wholly Jewish, under Jewish sovereignty or self-rule. After a period of tribal organization and government by Judges, a monarchy was set up by Saul in 1025 BCE. His successor David consolidated the kingdom and made Jerusalem its capital. About 930 BCE, on the death of his son Solomon, who built the Temple, the kingdom was split into the realms of Judah, in the south, and Israel, in the north.

The expansion of the Assyrian and Babylonian empires brought first Israel and later Judah under their sway, and many Jews were exiled to Babylon in 586 BCE, after the destruction of the First Temple. Repatriation in the days of Cyrus of Persia and the building of the Second Temple, 18 years later, marked the beginning of a period of revival and the creation of the Second Commonwealth.

For four centuries the Land of Israel enjoyed a large measure of self-rule under Persian and Hellenistic (Ptolemaic and Seleucid) tutelage. When in 168 BCE Seleucid Syria sought to interfere with that autonomy, the Jews rose in revolt under the Maccabees and regained a full independence which lasted over two centuries in the kingdom of the Hasmonaean and Herodian dynasties.

Towards the close of this period the Jews, in a series of uprisings and wars, defied Roman imperial might. Ultimately, in 70 CE, Rome subdued Judaea and destroyed the Second Temple, whose one remaining wall, the Western Wall, became a focus of pilgrimage.

After two generations, revolt flared up again and independence was briefly restored in 132 under the leadership of Simon Bar-Kochba. The Roman crushing of Jewish independence did not, however, dislodge the Jews from their Homeland. For centuries afterwards the country continued to be predominantly Jewish, and under Roman and Byzantine supremacy the Jews maintained and developed their autonomous legal and cultural institutions.

Upheld and fortified in dispersion by the messianic vision of an ultimate return, the Jews never forsook their Homeland or forgot their links with it.

Although the Temple was destroyed, the physical and spiritual nexus between the Jewish people and the Land of Israel was not broken. Throughout the succeeding centuries, even if a large part of the nation was driven from one exile to another, many stayed on, reinforced from time to time by returning exiles, maintaining their communities and settlements in the face of all manner of persecutions, natural disasters and alien conquests. For nearly two thousand years, they provided the nucleus around which the aspirations of the dispersed nation crystallized and, through them, the nation clung to the dream of returning to its Land.

The numerous invasions, conquests and counter-invasions which the country endured between the biblical period and the 19th century turned many parts of a once fertile, cultivated and wooded land into a desert. Yet, though so much of their Land was ravaged, the Jews clung stubbornly to their age-old roots in it. This volume is a tribute to those unforgettable generations, to the perpetuity of Jewish presence in the Land which they attest.

DAN BAHAT, an archaeologist, is a graduate of the Hebrew University of Jerusalem. He has participated in and headed many excavations all over the country. He is a member of the staff of the State of Israel's Department of Antiquities and Museums, as well as the Israel Museum in Jerusalem.

1st CENTURY

1.

2.

This was the last century of Jewish rule in Judaea, although at the same time Roman prefects were in governmental positions. The Jews constituted the majority of the population, enjoying religious independence and extensive autonomy until the outbreak of the Jewish revolt against Rome, in 66 CE. This was followed by the destruction of the Second Temple by Titus in 70 CE. The First Temple had been built by Solomon in approximately 940 BCE and destroyed by the Chaldeans in 586 BCE. The Second Temple was built by the Jews on their return from the Babylonian Exile, in 538 BCE, and enlarged and improved by Herod around 20 BCE.

1. *Hebrew inscription from the Second Temple period:"To the place of trumpeting . . ."*

The stone bearing the inscription is believed to have been located on top of the southwestern corner of the Temple Mount Wall, from where a priest would blow a trumpet to usher in the Sabbath, as is mentioned in contemporary sources.

2. *One of the Dead Sea Scrolls (rolled and unrolled). This one is Genesis Apocrypha discovered in 1947, containing a commentary on Genesis as interpreted by the sect inhabiting the western shore of the Dead Sea.*

1.

Under Roman rule, the Jews maintained considerable influence in government, and successfully opposed the appointment of Herod's son Archelaus to the governorship of Judaea.

Their military prowess was also such that they succeeded in continuing their struggle against the Romans for nearly three years (67–70 CE). The real significance of the Jewish

1. Copper coins discovered at Masada, which were struck by the independent Jewish government during the great revolt of 66–70 CE. The inscription reads: "2nd Year of the Independence of Zion", and, on the obverse, "Jerusalem the Sacred".

2. Part of the synagogue discovered at Masada This is the earliest known synagogue and was built by the Zealots who dwelled in Masada till its heroic fall in 73 CE.

3. General view of the northern end of the rock of Masada. The edifice was originally built by King Herod (37 BCE–4 BCE) as a desert fortress and palace, consisting of three terraces, storerooms and a large bath-house (all visible here), as well as fortifications and barracks. Later Masada served as a camp for about a thousand Jewish soldiers and their families who withstood an extended Roman siege. When the Romans were about to enter the palace the Jews decided to take their own lives. Only two women survived.

revolts lay in the fact that they greatly weakened the striking force of the Romans at a time when countries such as Babylon and Persia, which lay outside the Roman domain, presented a threat to the empire. Jews who lived in these countries supported the Jews of Judaea, forcing the Romans to take account of the links between the Jews living in their Homeland and the Jews in other countries which were hostile to Rome.

1. The Arch of Titus in the Roman forum. It was built by the emperor to commemorate his Judaean victory and shows the triumphal parade with the Temple vessels carried aloft. Conspicuous is the Temple menorah.

2. Part of the massive wall around the Cave of Machpelah in Hebron, where the Patriarchs are buried. In its present form it was built by Herod, using the methods employed in constructig the walls of the Temple in Jerusalem.

2ndCENTURY

During the period of the Second Temple, the Sanhedrin was the judicial body of the Jewish people and its 71-member Council was located in Jerusalem. After the destruction of the Second Temple, and the collapse of the national symbol of independence, Jewish political, economic and spiritual institutions continued to exist. The Sanhedrin was transferred in 70 CE from Jerusalem to Yavneh, where its authority was recognized by the Romans. Yavneh was now the focal point for all Diaspora Jewry, which was at that time scattered throughout Mesopo-

1.

1. *Marble screen found at Ashkelon, dating from the 2nd–3rd centuries CE and probably belonging to a synagogue.*

2. *After the destruction of the Second Temple the Jews tried to maintain their ceremonial religious life. While the Temple still stood services were performed by 24 priestly courses. After the destruction of the Temple these courses settled in Galilee. The courses and towns where they lived became the subjects of prayers and hymns for many centuries. This map shows the distribution of the courses, as based on their hymns.*

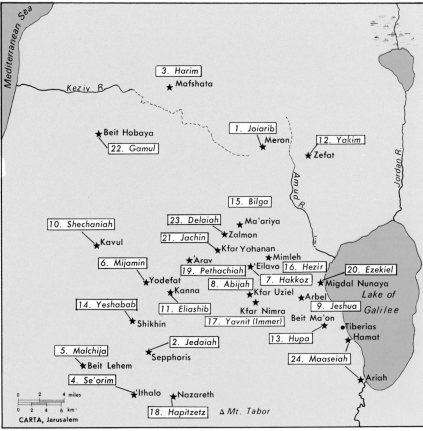

2.

8

1.

2.

3.

'tamia, Cyrenaica, Egypt, Cyprus and Asia Minor, until the reign of the Emperor Trajan (98–117 CE), when many communities were destroyed, following a revolt.

Under both the Hellenistic and the Roman regimes, attempts were made to force the Jewish community of the country to adopt non-Jewish customs and beliefs. A typical instance is the effort to introduce the worship of Caesar as a god. By endeavouring to hellenize the country, during Hadrian's rule (117–138), the occupiers brought upon themselves Bar-Kochba's protracted revolt (132–

1. *Coin struck during the brief rule of Bar-Kochba, showing the façade of the Temple which had been destroyed 65 years before. The inscription, in ancient Hebrew script, reads: "Simeon", the first name of Bar-Kochba.*

2. *Letter written by Bar-Kochba referring to administrative problems with his soldiers. It is one of many found at Wadi Muraba'at near the Dead Sea.*

3. *Archive found in the "Cave of Letters", discovered at Nahal Hever in the Judaean desert. It contains letters written by the commander of Ein Gedi during the Bar-Kochba revolt, as well as some dictated by Bar-Kochba himself.*

135). This was undoubtedly the climactic event of the century for the Jews. The revolt failed, those of its leaders who had not died in the war (Bar-Kochba fell at Betar) were condemned to death, many villages were destroyed and Jerusalem was rebuilt as a Roman-pagan city named Aelia Capitolina, after Aelius Hadrianus. The name of the country was changed to Syria-Palaestina by the Romans.

"Julius Severus was deterred from engaging the enemy (i.e., the Jews) in face to face combat as their numbers were so large."
(*Dio Cassius*, Book LXIX)

1.

1. *Clay oil lamps from the period after the destruction of the 2nd Temple. The lamps are decorated with such Jewish symbols as lulav and etrog.*

2. *Prayer shawl (tallith) found in the "Cave of Letters" in the Judaean desert. Though differing from those used today, the one in the picture bears the typical markings of prayer shawls.*

2.

1.

3rd CENTURY

During this century the Mishnah was formally arranged, its laws indicating the extent of independence allowed to the Jews in the Land of Israel. The final form of this body of ancient traditions and customs was drawn up in this century by Rabbi Judah Hanassi, the President.

1. *The village of Naveh on the Golan Heights has many buildings constructed by its former Jewish inhabitants, who settled the area extensively in the 3rd century CE. The house shown here dates from that time and its lintel depicts a menorah, vines, leaves, etc.*

2. *A corner of cave no. 3 in the Great Catacombs at Beth She'arim (Lower Galilee). The wall relief shows a man with a menorah on his head. This cemetery served as a burial centre for the Jews of Eretz Israel and the Diaspora during the 3rd and 4th centuries CE.*

3. *Carved lintel from a Jewish building at Dabbura on the Golan. The Hebrew inscription reads: "This is the Beth Midrash [talmudic academy] of Rabbi Eliezer Hakappar." Eliezer or Eleazar Hakappar is a late second-century CE Sage, and is mentioned in the Talmud.*

2.

3.

The position of President of the Jewish population had come into existence immediately after the destruction of the Second Temple. It endured until the year 429, when Emperor Theodosius II took away all authority from the office occupied at the time by Rabbi Gamaliel VI. The President was also the presiding judge of the Sanhedrin (supreme judicial body), a dual function covering every aspect of the spiritual and secular life of the people. He always came from the House of Hillel, which was descended from the House of David, so that both in the Holy Land and in exile the Jews regarded him as their natural ruler and the last vestige of their former independent State. His spiritual power was so great that the Romans themselves sought his cooperation, giving the Jews the task of tax collection and the rights to ownership of large areas of land. The rule of the President resembled that of a king, including the power to pass the death sentence.

One of the best known synagogues excavated is that of Capernaum on the northern shore of the Sea of Galilee. The local community appears to have been very prosperous and the synagogue marks the zenith of Jewish art in Eretz Israel. The two examples of decorative art shown here depict (above) a menorah with incense burner (left) and ritual horn, shofar (right), on a capital; (below) an architectonic block representing apples, pomegranates, leaves, etc.

1.

2.

After the Bar-Kochba revolt the spiritual centre passed from Yavneh to Usha, Beth She'arim and Sepphoris, in Galilee, because of the existence of a large Jewish community in that region. There is evidence that a smaller community existed in Judaea. During the middle of the century the spiritual centre moved to Tiberias. At this time Roman power in the Land was temporarily weak, owing to the conflict with Persia and Palmyra, which ended only two centuries later. This was an age of considerable synagogue building in Galilee, providing evidence of the artistic talents and prosperity of the Galilaean Jews. Diocletian (284–305) restored order in the Land, enabling the Jewish community to flourish.

1. The similar façades of synagogues in Meron and Kfar Bar'am.

2. Three inscriptions discovered in Dabbura on the Golan Heights. These inscriptions are a few of many more discovered at that village. The three inscriptions form part of an inscribed cornice. It reads "Elazar the son of Raba has donated the columns above the arch and the roof beams"; at the bottom of the 3rd part is the name of the actual builder—"Isitkos". All the inscriptions indicate the existence of a Jewish village on the Golan in the 2nd and 3rd centuries CE.

4th CENTURY

During this century the Roman empire was divided into two parts and Judaea became part of the eastern (Byzantine) empire, with Christianity, under the rule of Constantine, the established religion. Eusebius (260–339), an ecclesiastical historian, who was probably born in Judaea and was bishop of Caesarea, has left detailed accounts of the Jewish community in the country at that time, making specific mention of a number of villages in the south, such as: Ein Gedi, Eshtamoa (today: Samu'), Yutta (today: Yata).

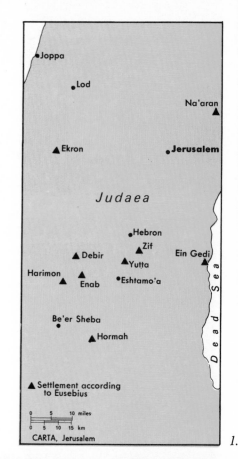

1.

1. Map showing the Jewish communities mentioned by the Church Father Eusebius, in the southern mountains of Judaea. These villages probably continued to exist until the Islamic conquest.

2. Very little now remains of what were once flourishing Jewish communities in Eretz Israel. Most of our knowledge of the past is derived from excavations. In the small village of Eshtamoa, however, the Arab inhabitants live in 1800-year-old houses which were built by their Jewish predecessors. One of the relics of the past still evident in the village is this stone with a menorah carved on it, dating from the 3rd century CE.

2.

14

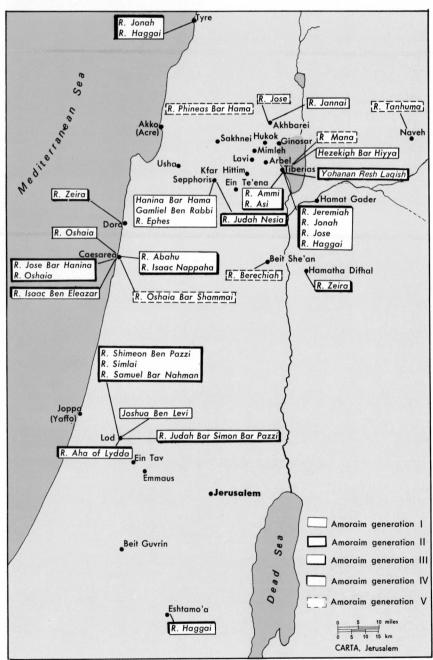

About the town of Lydda he reports:

"In the Holy Land there is a large town with a considerable population consisting only of Jews, called in Aramaic, Lod (Lydda), and in Greek, Diocaesarea."
(*Eusebius, History of the Martyrs of Palestine*, p. 29.)

According to St. Jerome, a Church Father who lived in Bethlehem (384–420) and is famous for his translation of the Bible into Latin, there was a Jewish community in Jerusalem and the general economic position of the Jews was such that Julian the Apostate (361–363) regarded them as a counterweight to Christianity. The

1. *A stone on which a menorah is carved. This stone and many other Jewish artistic relics were found in buildings in the village of Naveh on the Golan Heights. The menorah is flanked by shofars and a lulav (cf. above p. 17.)*

2. *Map showing the places where the Amoraim dwelt. These were the spiritual leaders of the nation after the decline of the Presidency. For convenience sake they are classified according to the period in which they lived: 1st generation – 225-260; 2nd generation – 260-290; 3rd generation – 290-320; 4th generation – 320-360; 5th generation – 360-400. The Amoraim lived and taught in a number of Jewish communities and on the basis of the lists mentioning their names and towns we are able to trace the location of some of the important communities which existed then in the country.*

15

1.

revolt against Gallus, in the year 351, is described thus:

"Gallus persecuted the Jews, who slaughtered his entire garrison in the night and afterwards declared open revolt. He (Gallus) killed thousands of people, even infants, and destroyed the towns of Caesarea, Tiberias and Lydda and set fire to many others." (*St. Jerome (Hieronymus), Chronicon* p. 238.)

1. Passage from the Book of Isaiah, 66:14. "And when ye see this your heart shall rejoice, and your bones shall flourish like an herb", a passage which was interpreted by many commentators as referring to the redemption and national revival. The passage is carved on one of the stones of the Western Wall of the Temple platform in Jerusalem. It was inscribed by a Jew during the 4th century when the Emperor Julian allowed Jews to resettle in Jerusalem and to rebuild places of worship in 361–363 CE.

2. A fragment of the mosaic floor of Hamath near Tiberias. On the site there are three successive synagogues, one above the other. This fragment belongs to the 4th century. The middle panel shows the Zodiac, and in the corners the four seasons are represented. In our fragment one can see Spring represented as a maiden holding a basket containing the fruits of that season.

2.

1.

2.

5th CENTURY

During the period following the accession of Theodosius I to the imperial throne, in 379, the monks conducted intensive missionary activities in an attempt to counterbalance the strength of the non-Christians, who had flourished during the reign of Julian the Apostate. The fifth century marks the end of the Hellenistic world; few non-Christian communities remained, apart from the Jews. Theodosius I did not persecute the Jews but his grandson Theodosius II (408–450) yielded entirely to the demands of the Church. The Jews were deprived of their relative autonomy and of their right to hold public positions. The Jewish courts were forbidden to sit on mixed Jewish-Christian cases and construction of new synagogues was prohibited.

Christians became the majority of the population in the Land of Israel and the Jews were forbidden to enter Jerusalem except on one day a year to mourn the destruction of the Temple.

1. A part of a mosaic floor from the synagogue of Usfiyah (on Mount Carmel): it shows a wreath surrounding the inscription "Peace upon Israel". The synagogue which was excavated in 1933 is dated to the second half of the 5th century CE.

2. A part of a mosaic floor discovered in 1953 at Hulda. The floor has a framed panel, bearing the inscription "Blessing upon the nation". One can distinguish a menorah and other ritual objects such as lulav, etrog, and shofar.

In St. Jerome's Commentary to the Book of Zephaniah, we read:

"To this day it is forbidden to the unbelievers (i.e., the Jews) to come to Jerusalem. Only for the purpose of mourning are they allowed to come and then must purchase a permit to weep for the destruction of their kingdom . . . Even their tears must be bought. On the anniversary of the destruction of the city by the Romans one could see the unhappy people gather together, old men and old women, the infirm and the weak, all dressed in rags . . ."

During this period, the leadership of the Jews appears to have passed to the Jewish councils sitting throughout the country, which had been divided at the end of the third century into two provinces by the Romans. In 443 the Empress Eudoxia settled in Jerusalem, arousing unfounded hopes among the Jews that the day of deliverance was approaching.

Towards the end of the century, construction of synagogues was renewed, though the legal background for this is unclear. It seems, however, that the Jews benefitted from the lax observance of laws forbidding the erection of synagogues all over the country, e.g., in Tiberias, Beth Alpha, Beth She'an and Maon (Nirim).

A letter dated 438 from the heads of the Galilaean Jews to the Jewish community in Egypt expresses the

1. A fragment of the mosaic floor of a synagogue at Gerasa (Trans-Jordan). The fragment shows pairs of animals entering Noah's ark. The menorah is surrounded by a Greek inscription which reads "(Dedicated) to His holy place, Amen, Selah, Peace upon the community." A Christian church built on the foundations of the synagogue should therefore be dated to the 4th or 5th century CE.

2. This map indicates the number of synagogues that existed between the first and sixth century C.E. Their distribution represents the diffusion of the Jews throughout the country.

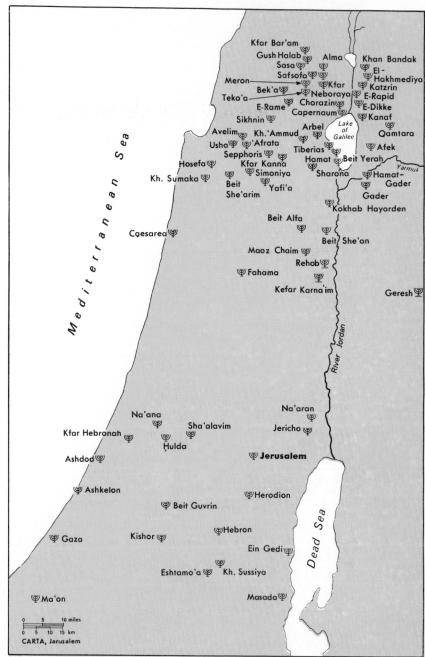

yearning of the Jewish inhabitants of the country for the revival of their kingdom. Here is a quotation from the letter:

"To the great and mighty Jewish people; from the priests and elders in Galilee — many greetings!

"Know that the end of the exile of our people is near and all our tribes shall be gathered together. Lo, the Rulers of Rome have decreed that our city, Jerusalem, shall be returned to us. Come quickly to Jerusalem for the Feast of Tabernacles, for our kingdom is at hand in Jerusalem."

(From a Chronicle composed by the Syrian monk Bar-Yoma, published in *Revue de l'Orient Chrétien 1913–1914*.)

Literary activity, despite the fact that the Jews were deprived of their political independence, never dwindled. In this century, the Jerusalem Talmud and several homiletic collections were written or completed, the best-known of them being the Tanhuma, and the "Great Midrash" (Midrash Rabba).

During the 3rd century, Jewish scholars began to compile the traditions and interpretations of the Mishnah (biblically-derived jurisprudence), which in turn became the core of the Jerusalem Talmud ("Book of Study"), an assembly of juridical, religious and sociological material relating to the Jewish community after the Roman conquest. The talmudic compilation ends in the 5th century.

1. Marble screen found at Ashdod and belonging to a 5th-century synagogue.

2. Tombstone from Zoar on the south-eastern shore of the Dead Sea, dating from 450 CE. Inscription reads "Tombstone of Esther, daughter of Adio, who passed away in the year 382 after the destruction of the Temple. Peace, peace be upon Israel."

3. "The monument (tombstone) of Justus the son of Isidoros, a member of the (county) council lived for . . . years." This tombstone found at Tiberias is dated around the 5th century. There was a great Jewish cemetery in Tiberias, mentioned by, among others, Gentile writers such as Epiphanius.

4. Stone found in a burial cave at Zippori in Lower Galilee. At the centre is the head of a nail by which the stone was attached to the rock. The inscription reads "Rabbi Yossa (Joseph) the Pale". Found in 1930, it is now in the Hebrew University of Jerusalem.

6th CENTURY

Tiberias now served as the seat of the main centre of learning and spiritual life of the country. The leading personality was Zutta, who had fled to the Land of Israel from Persia. His father, also called Zutta, had been a remarkable man, leading the Jews during the Babylonian Exile. He had been so adept at exploiting the political situation in Babylon that he had managed to set up an independent Jewish State there, lasting seven years (495–502). He was eventually crucified by Karad, the king of Persia.

The Yeshiva, the principal seat of learning in the country, was the unquestioned authority on all Jewish matters. Its constant removals from place to place are gloomy and incontestable evidence of the pressure under which it functioned.

1–2. Two examples of mosaic synagogue floors. The upper one, dating from the 6th century, is at Beth Alpha. The naive rural art makes an interesting contrast to the more sophisticated work in the lower picture. The latter dates from the 4th century and was found at the hot springs resort of Tiberias which was frequented by the rich. The sophisticated drawing of the Zodiac in the lower picture portrays the sun as a Greek god, possibly Apollo, while in the upper mosaic the sun is crudely drawn in the image of a chariot driver.

1.

2.

1.

2.

The Byzantine chronicler, John Malalas (491–578), who wrote a world history named *Chronographia*, records the story of the Jewish and Samaritan insurrection in 556. Thus he says:

"In the month of July the Samaritans and the Jews joined together against the Emperor of Palestine and made a bond."
(*Chronographia*, p. 455.)

Antoninus the Martyr, a Christian pilgrim who visited Palestine, apparently at the end of the 6th century, wrote:

"Nazareth! So great is the beauty of the Jewish women in the town that you will not find more beautiful women amongst the Jews in the length and breadth of this Land."

1. *Part of an inscription on the mosaic floor of a synagogue in Hamath-Gadar on the Yarmuk River. Because of its hot springs the site was visited by Jews from all parts of the country, who donated funds for the construction of the synagogue. The inscription reads: "May Ada, son of Tanhum, son of Monica, be remembered for good for donating a third of a dinar, and Yossa, son of Krozza and Monica, who donated half a dinar for this mosaic floor. May a blessing be upon them. Amen, selah, peace."*

2. *A mosaic panel from the floor of a synagogue at Na'aran in the Jericho plain. This panel shows two gazelles flanking a bush. Part of the panel was destroyed and restored in antiquity. It dates from the 5th or 6th century CE.*

21

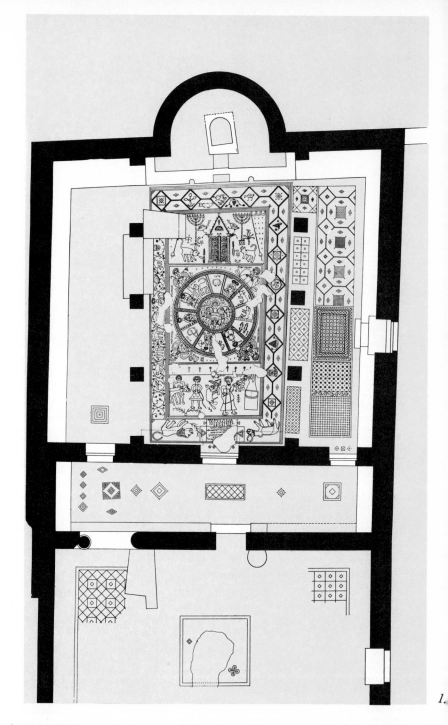

1. General plan of the synagogue at Beth
Alpha. Although the inhabitants of this
village were peasants they nevertheless
mobilised their resources in order to erect
this magnificent building in the 6th century
CE. It was destroyed in the 7th century and
all trace of it disappeared until it was found
by chance by members of Kibbutz Hefzibah
during the course of development works. It
was excavated by the Hebrew University of
Jerusalem in 1928. The plan shows the main
hall, the area occupied by the ark, the
entrance hall and the open courtyard. Its
mosiac floor is considered to be the best
example of peasant art from the end of the
Byzantine period.

2. Upper part of the mosaic floor found in
a syangogue at Maon in the western Negev,
depicting a menorah, ritual horn (shofar)
and other traditional objects. The entire
floor is decorated with a variety of animals
in a style typical of the 6th century.

7th CENTURY

At the beginning of this century, the Persians were advancing on the Byzantine province of Palestine. The Jews looked to the Persians, who had succeeded in preserving their independence in the face of Roman and Byzantine power, for salvation. Hoping to be permitted to worship freely once the Byzantine oppression had been removed, the Jews of Galilee joined with the Persian invaders, helped in conquering Acre and participated in the successful siege of Jerusalem. Contemporary accounts describe the assistance given by the Jews to the Persians. The Jewish community which was allowed to settle and worship in Jerusalem remained there for only a few years (614–617) until the Persians expelled the Jews from Jerusalem. Persian rule in the country ended in 629.

Euthychius, the Patriarch of Alexandria (d. 939), in his book of history tells:

"The Persian commander went to Damascus and destroyed the Land, and the Jews from Tiberias, Hebron, Nazareth and Tyre gathered together to help the Persians in destroying the Gentiles . . . and when Damascus was free from the Byzantine armies and the Persians gathered near Constantinople, the Jews of Jerusalem, Hebron, Tiberias, Damascus and Cyprus came together until they numbered 20,000 and came to Tyre to destroy it."
(*Annals of Euthychius I*, 216.)

وهى مدينة الجبارين التى تقدم ذكرها عند قصة سيدنا موسى عليه
السلام كما تقدم ذكره وهى شرقى بيت المقدس بالقرب من نهر الاردن
وكان النبى صلى الله عليه وسلم قد أخرج اليهود من المدينة فخرجوا الى
الشام والى أذرعات وأريحا ثم أجلى آخرهم عمر من الخطاب رضى الله
عنه فى امارته من أرض الحجاز الى تيماء وأريحا وقد صارت أريحا فى هذه
الازمنة قرية من قرى بيت المقدس وهى اقطاع لمن يكون نائبا بالقدس
الشريف ومن عجيب الاتفاق انها كانت من زمن بنى اسرائيل سكن
الجبارين وفى زمن الاسلام مختصة بحاكم الشرطة * ذكر نابلس روى
المشرف بسنده عن كعب * قال أحب البلاد الى الله الشام وأحب الشام
الى الله تعالى القدس وأحب القدس الى الله تعالى جبل نابلس ليأتين
على الناس زمان يتماسحونه بالجبال بينهم ونابلس مدينة بالارض
المقدسة مقابل بيت المقدس من جهة الشمال مسافتها عنه نحو يومين
بسير الاثقال خرج منها كثير من العلماء الاعيان وهى كثيرة العيون
والاشجار والفواكه ومعظم الاشجار بها وأحمها الزيتون وبها كثير من
السامرة فانهم يعتقدون ان القدس جبل نابلس وقد كذبوا خالفوا
جميع الامم فى ذلك لعنهم الله وقد قيل ان سيدنا يوسف عليه السلام قبر
بالقرب من نابلس وتقدم ذلك عند ذكره عليه السلام وبمدينة نابلس
مشهد بقال إن به أولاد يعقوب عليهم السلام أجمعين ويضواحيها
مشاهد كثيرة تنسب الى جماعة من الانبياء عليهم السلام *

A page from "The History of Jerusalem and Hebron" by the Moslem judge Mujir al-Din which relates that when the prophet Muhammad drove out the Jews of al-Medina (625) they emigrated to Syria, mostly to Adru'at (Der'aa) and Jericho. Later, the Caliph Omar b. al-Khattab expelled the Jews from the Hejaz to Taima' (now in northern Saudi Arabia) and Jericho, during the time of his reign (634–644).

However, when Heraclius, the Byzantine emperor, returned to Palestine in 629, the Jews welcomed him gladly, having been persecuted by the Persians.

"When Heraclius came to Tiberias, all the Jews that dwelt there in the mountains of Galilee and Nazareth and in every village in Galilee welcomed him with gifts and blessings and asked of him that he should protect them and seal this with a contract."
(*Annals of Euthychius II, 5.*)

Heraclius signed a treaty with them, guaranteeing to protect them and to take no revenge on them for their co-operation with the Persians. He broke this agreement under pressure from the Christian priests in Jerusalem.

With the rise of Islam, the friendly ties which Muhammad had sought to foster with the Jews, due to his adoption of many Jewish principles of cult and belief, were not established. Nevertheless, the Moslem conquest of the country in 638 CE was favourable to the Jews; settlement in Jerusalem was resumed and the Jews were appointed guardians of the Temple Mount in return for their aid to the conquering army.

A letter discovered in the Cairo Genizah — a collection of letters, fragments of holy books and other writings hidden since the 11th century in a synagogue of Cairo and discovered there in the 19th century — tells of an agreement between the Second Caliph and the Jews (in 638) by which seventy families from Tiberias, where there had been a Jewish community throughout the Byzantine period, were allowed to settle in the southern part of Jerusalem.

In Hebron, too, the Jews were rewarded for aiding the Moslems by being granted permission to live under conditions of *protection*, the custom-

2.

1. *Seven-branched candlestick, one several painted in red on the plaster wall o building dating from the 7th century C This building stands in the area of the which forms the southern corner of Temple Mount. Here an attempt was ma by Jews to rebuild the Temple after p mission was granted them by the Persi who wrested Eretz Israel from Byzantines (614 CE). This permission u later rescinded after the Persians reached understanding with the Byzantines.*

2. *In the debate held between the Cali Omar and Sophronius, Patriarch and lea of the surrendered Christian community Jerusalem, as to the conditions of su mission, the question of non-admission the Jews to Jerusalem was discussed to Omar, wishing to repay the Jews for th help in the Moslem conquest of Palesti demanded that 200 families be permitted inhabit the town. The Patriarch refus obstinately. Finally, there was agreement 70 families who were allowed to dwell in t city.*
This document from the Cairo Geniza written in Judaeo-Arabic, tells the story that dispute.

ary status of non-Moslems in Moslem countries. They were also allowed to build a synagogue in front of the entrance to the Cave of Machpelah where, according to Jewish and Moslem tradition, the Patriarchs and their wives are buried.

"But when the Arabs who came to Hebron marvelled at the strength and beauty of the wall (that surrounded the Cave of Machpelah) and at the fact that there was no opening through which it was possible to enter, some Jews who had remained under the Greek rule approached them, saying: 'Protect us so that we may live under like conditions amongst you and permit us to build a synagogue in front of the entrance to the cave, and we will then show you at what place you should instal the gate and so it was done.' "
(*Canonici Hebronensis Tractatus de inventione sanctorum patriarcharum Abraham, Ysaac et Jacob.*)

Jewish communities lived in the south of the country. The synagogue at Sussiya remained standing until the 9th or 10th century in contrast to other synagogues which were either destroyed during the 7th century or were forsaken by their worshippers. In Eilat, at the northern end of the Red Sea, Muhammad made a treaty with the Jewish community similar to those made with other non-Moslem groups.

This era of Moslem conquest and the rule of the Ummayads was a time of peace for the Jews. However, conditions did not improve for the Jews in other Arab countries and they were expelled either during the period of Muhammad or afterwards. The Jews expelled from Khaibar and Fadak in the northern Hijaz journeyed across to Transjordan (Der'aa) and to Jericho. (Mujir al-Din, ed., *History of Jerusalem and Hebron*, 1496, p. 423.)

1. A part of the mosaic floor from the synagogue of Jericho. The floor is covered in geometrical designs. In its centre it has a circle with a menorah flanked by a shofar and a lulav, below which the inscription "Peace upon Israel" can be read.

2. The Arab geographer Yaqut (d. 1229) when mentioning Eilat in his geographical dictionary discusses the real contents of the pact signed between Muhammad and the Jews of Eilat (then: Aylah). The discussion tries to elucidate what are the true obligations imposed on the Jewish citizens of that town, due to the new orders of later Caliphs.

8th CENTURY

The Ummayads (661–750) were followed by the Abbasids who founded Baghdad and made it their capital. Their rule in the country lasted 120 years. The focal point of the Jewish community in the country, the Yeshiva, moved from Tiberias to Jerusalem as a result of an earthquake in Galilee in 748. Michael the Syrian relates that thirty synagogues in Tiberias were destroyed. St. Willibald, a pilgrim from Britain, verifies the number of synagogues in Tiberias.

The Jewish community in Jerusalem continued to flourish and Jews were among those who guarded the walls of the Dome of the Rock. In return they were absolved from paying the poll-tax imposed on all non-Moslems. The Jews were employed in clearing the Haram area of waste.

Inscription recently found at Sussiya in southern Judaea. Though the original name of the village is unknown, the inscription, which comes from the synagogue there, indicates the existence of a Jewish community as late as the 8th century.
"Remember for good and blessing . . .
that strengthened and did . . .
the second day of the week . . . year.
four thousand . . .
from the creation of the world . . .
. . . Let there be peace."

1.

2.

There is also documentary evidence that other Jews made the glass and wicks for the oil lamps and that these were the traditional occupations of the Jews of Jerusalem from the 8th century onwards (Mujir al-Din, *History of Jerusalem and Hebron*, p. 249).

There was a Jewish community in Gaza, led by Rabbi Moshe of Gaza, the Masorite (*masora*, the correct vocalization of the Pentateuch, was studied by the scholars of this period).

With the rise of the Abbasids, relations between Moslems and non-Moslems (both Jews and Christians) deteriorated. Non-Moslems had to wear a special badge. Increasing discrimination — social and economic — against non-Moslems caused many Jews to move to Fustat (Old Cairo) to establish a new community there.

1. *Installation for dyeing clothes in the area south-west of the Temple Mount. It dates from the 8th century CE. During this period Jews were brought by the Moslems to work on the Temple Mount. Among various types of work which the Jews did, dyeing material was one of the important crafts entrusted to them. The Moslems allowed the Jews to live in the Temple Mount area.*

2. *A lane in the old town of Ramla, founded by the Ummayads, which served as capital of the country. Jewish presence here was continuous until later mediaeval times.*

27

1. *Among the many examples of Islamic architecture found in Eretz Israel, the building known as Hisham's Palace is one of the most famous. It was built at Jericho as a winter resort for the Ummayad Caliphs and was decorated with consummate skill. While still under construction it was destroyed by an earthquake. This Hebrew abecedaire, probably inscribed by one of the workers on the building, is one of the most interesting finds from the palace. The existence of Jewish builders, masons and other craftsmen is significant since we know very little about the Jews of Jericho during the 8th century.*

.2. *A page from the "History of Jerusalem and Hebron" composed (1496) by the Moslem judge Mujir al-Din which relates that "The Dome of the Rock was kept by the Jewish servants on whom a poll-tax was not levied. They worked at cleaning the Haram (the Temple Mount). There are also Jewish servants who make the glass, lamps, vessels, candlesticks, etc. They too are exempted from the poll-tax, as well as those who prepare the straw for the threads of the lamps. This exemption was given to them and their offspring from the time of Abd Al-Malik (d. 705) and thenceforth."*

ماتاسلراوفيه من الصهاريج أربعة وعشرون صهريجا كبارا وفيـه من
المنابر أربعة ثلاثة منها صف واحد غربي المسجد وواحدة على باب
الاسباط وكان له من الخدم اليهود الذين لا يؤخذ منهم جزية عشرة رجال
وتوالدوا نصاروا عشرين لكنس أوساخ المسجد الناشئ في المواسم
والشتاء والصيف ولكنس المطاهر التي حول الجامع وله من الخدم
النصارى عشرة أهل بيت يتوارثون خدمته لعمل الحصر ولكنس حصر
المسجد وكنس القناة التي يجري فيها الماء الى الصهاريج وكنس
الصهاريج أيضا وغير ذلك وله من الخدم اليهود جماعة يعملون الزجاج
القناديل والاقداح والتريات وغير ذلك لا يؤخذ منهم جزية ولا من
الذين يقومون بالقش لفتائل القناديل جاريا عليهم وعلى أولادهم أبدا
ماتاسلموا من عهد عبد الملك بن مروان وهلم جرا * وتوفي عبد الملك بن
مروان بدمشق في يوم الخميس لخمس عشرة ليلة مضت من رمضان سنة
ست وثمانين من الهجرة الشريفة وعمره ستون سنة وكانت خلافته منذ
قتل ابن الزبير واجتماع الناس له ثلاث عشرة سنة وأربعة أشهر تنقص
سبع ليال وكان بالشام وما والاها قبل قتل ابن الزبير بسبع سنين ونحو
تسعة أشهر ومات الحجاج في شهر رمضان وقيل شوال سنة خمس
وتسعين للهجرة وله ثلاث وخمسون سنة وكان موته بواسط وهو الذي
بناها وأخفى قبره واجرى عليه الماء * ومات رجاء بن حماة الذي تولى بناء
الصخرة والمسجد الاقصى في سنة اثنى عشرة ومائة وكان رأسه أحمر
ولحيته حمراء * ولما ولى سليمان بن عبد الملك الاموي الخلافة بعد أخيه
الوليد في سنة ست وتسعين من الهجرة أتى بيت المقدس وأتته الوفود
بالبيعة فلم يرو فادة كانت أهنى من الوفادة اليه فكان يجلس في قبة في صحن
مسجد بيت المقدس مما يلي الصخرة ولعلها القبة المعروفة بقبة سليمان عند
باب الدويدارية وبسط البسط بين يدي قبته علم المنارف والكراسي

9th CENTURY

The Abbasid dynasty, which ruled from Baghdad until 1258, neglected its western provinces, directing most of its efforts towards strengthening its position in Iraq and constructing and reinforcing the capital and its environs.

Since the central rule was weak and inefficient, Beduin tribes from southern Transjordan succeeded in penetrating the cultivated land, imposing their rule on the inhabitants. Until the Beduin penetration, which increased in the 10th century, the Arab population had not made its mark on the towns of the country. Arab geographers, such as Yaqubi (891), make repeated mention of places of mixed population, among them Ramla and Yavneh, comprising Persians, Samaritans and Jews. As Beduin power grew, with the occupation of the town of Ramla in 1025, villages were abandoned, and the population concentrated principally in the larger towns; the older, mixed population of the villages was rapidly superseded by the Arab-Beduin element.

After the Six Day War a group of Hebrew inscriptions and drawings were found in southern Sinai, apparently indicating the existence of Jewish merchants who engaged in trade between Arabia and the Western world. Their knowledge of Hebrew indicates a probable connection with the Jews of the Holy Land.

Mediterranean Sea

Akhziv
Kabrata
Elkosh
Mafshata
Kfar Bar'am
Gush Halav
Sufsaf
Dalton
Kfar Sima'el
Kfar Neborya
Yanuh
Meron
Zefat
Shazor
Beit Parod
'Akhbari
Akko
Dagan
Kfar
Chorazin
Kfar Nahum
Sha'ab
Ma'ariya
Hannanya
Kamtara
Kabul
Zalmon
Hurok
Mimlah
Migdal Nunia
Kfar Tamrata
Sakhney
Kfar Nimra
Evlayim
Kfar
Kfar Hittin
Kurshi
Shefar'am
Mandi
Mashkana
Arbel
Afek
Yusha
Rimon
Tiberias
Beit Me'on
'Ardascus
Zippori
Lubaei
Kfar Manor
Tiv'on
Kann'a
Adami
Sargoniya
'Aithalo
Nazareth
Kfar Agon
Yarmuk
Simoniya
Yafi'a
Daverat
Zemah
Hamat Gader
Gevat
Ginnegar
Tarbenet
Gebal
Edrei
Shunem
Kokhav
Arbel
Beit She'an

Asher

Geresh

Jordan R

Darela

Kfah Saba

Kfar Kasem
Adam
Datha
Bnei Berak
Ono
Shilo
Kfar Pegai
Tur Shim'on
Yafo
Lod
Hadid
Gophna
Modi'in
Beit-El
Gimzo
Kharruba
Dorin
Beit Horon
Mikhmas
Jericho
Yavne
Emmaus
Ekron
Ashdod

⊚ **Jerusalem**

Beithar
Bethlehem
Medeba

Ashkelon

Beit Guvrin

Dead Sea

Beror Hayil

Gaza

Yutta
Ein Gedi
Kfar Aziz
Eshtamo'a
Carmel
Ma'on

5   10 miles
5   10   15 km
© Carta, Jerusalem

This century witnessed the beginnings of a Karaite settlement in Jerusalem which continued to expand during the next hundred years.

The tendency of the Jews in the Land of Israel to detach themselves from the cultural centre in Babylonia and to maintain spiritual and religious independence was expressed in the debate about the right to fix the dates of the festivals. This right was claimed by the Rosh Ha-Havura (Head of the Association), the principal of the religious academy in the Land. Spiritual leaders in Babylonia yielded to the superiority of the Jews in the Homeland in this matter.

2.

1. *This map provides a listing of Jewish communities from the 9th century whose ancient Hebrew names are evident in the Arabic names they came to be known by.*

2. *A fragment of the mosaic floor of the synagogue of the village of Sussiya in South Judaea. The floor which shows many designs was renovated more than once. The panel shown here belongs to the latest period when the synagogue was used and should be dated to the 8th or even 9th century CE. The inscription reads: "Should be remembered for good and blessing our Master, His Holiness, R. Issi the Cohen, the Respected, the son of Rabbi who has donated this mosaic and plastered and white-washed its (the synagogue's) wall as he promised at the banquet of his son, R. Johanan the Cohen, the Scribe. 'Peace upon Israel'."*

10ᵗʰ CENTURY

In 969, power in the Holy Land was seized by the Fatimids, who reigned until the Crusader conquest of 1099. Several counsellors of Jewish origin served in their Egyptian capital, Cairo.

Taxation and persecution compelled the Jews to leave their rural communities and move to the towns. Even in the towns their situation hardly improved, however.

The elders of the Jerusalem community wrote in 1058 to the Jews of the Diaspora:

" And there is no mercy but that we gather and bow down and beg for return to Jerusalem in mercy."
(From a document found in the *Cairo Genizah*.)

Our most important source of information for the history of the Jewish community in the 8th–11th centuries CE is what is known as the Genizah (archives) of Cairo. Many books, documents and other written material were kept for safety in a synagogue there. Nothing was added after the 11th century. Upon the discovery of the Genizah in the 19th century, the vast collection, numbering thousands of documents, was distributed throughout the museums of the world. Most of them, such as letters written from Eretz Israel to Egypt, describe the Jewish community of Eretz Israel. The scrolls shown here and on p. 33 form sections of a guidebook to Jerusalem, written in Arabic in Hebrew letters by a Jew. It was probably written during the first half of the 10th century when Jews were still permitted to pray at one of the gates to the Temple Mount.

Many Jews were cloth-dyers, tanners and metalsmiths. This period saw the decline of the *Geonim* (the principals of the academies) in the Land of Israel during post-talmudic times.

In the southern part of the country there were small Jewish communities. A Christian historian, Yahya ibn Said Atantaki, in his *Continuation to the Annals of Euthychius,* refers to the existence of a Jewish community in Ashkelon.

The Jerusalem-born Arab geographer Muqaddasi, who wrote his book in 985, complains that in Jerusalem the

"Learned men are few and the Christians numerous, and the same are unmannerly in public places . . . Study councils remain unvisited and erudite men have no renown; the schools are unattended for there are no lectures. Everywhere the Christians and the Jews have the upper hand, and the mosque is void of either congregation or assembly of learned men."
(Muqaddasi, *Knowledge of Climes,* p. 167.)

Muqaddasi also notes that the Jews were employed as official money-changers, dyers and tanners. There were Jewish communities in the north

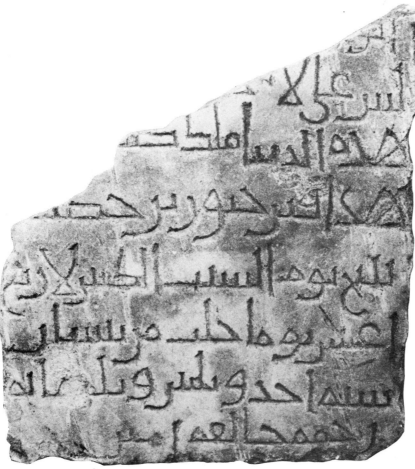

A fragment of a Jewish epitaph found in Ramla, commemorating a man named Hayyun who died on the Great Sabbath (the Saturday before Passover) on the fourteenth of Nisan in the year 331 AH (943 CE).

of the country in Acre, Gush-Halav and Dalton. Those who lived near Lake Hula wove mats and ropes.

In Tiberias, the Jewish community specialised in the traditional manner of reciting, cantillating and interpreting the Scriptures. Several generations of the Ben Asher family are documented as having lived there. The most prominent Masorite of that family was Aharon ben Moses ben Asher (d. 960), author of a Masoretic textbook, *Dikdukei Hateamim*. The vocalization of the script had been started in the 8th century, and this development ranks among the most important cultural and creative achievements of the period, having a profound influence on later Jewish thought and literature. A 10th century source tells us:

"No one was left in this generation who dealt with the syntax and grammar of the language. Amongst the people of Isfahan, Basra, Tustar and others, there was no one who did not prefer the style of Eretz Israel, and even those amongst the elders who did not read according to the fashion of Eretz Israel but read according to the Babylonian fashion and knew the readings of Eretz Israel only by hearsay, even they, if they wished to discuss matters of syntax and grammar, would have spoken only about the Eretz Israel style and no other."
(From *The Book of Lights and Watchtowers* by the 10th century Karaite, Kirkisani [a treatise on religious law].)

The work of the vocalizers and grammarians of Eretz Israel came to a halt only in the tenth century. Aharon ben-Asher and Moshe ben-Naphthali, who lived and worked in Tiberias in the middle of the tenth century, are considered to have been the last of the Masorites. The different textual versions of their writings engaged the attention of grammarians for a long time, and the disciples of these two scholars recorded the conclusions of their masters. The following is a copy of a passage from the manuscript in which these changes are recorded.

There was a continuous flow to Jerusalem of Jews from various countries, seeking shelter. We learn this from a letter sent by one of the elders of the Karaite community to the Egyptian Diaspora:

"And know that Jerusalem at this time is a sanctuary to all who seek shelter, and gives rest to all who mourn, and comforts all who are poor and in want, and all the servants of the Lord come into her from every family and from every city, and amongst them women weeping and wailing in the holy tongue and in the Persian tongue and in the tongue of Ishmael. Men and women dressed in sack-cloth and ashes . . . and they go up to the Mount of Olives all who are heavy of heart and in pain."
(From a letter written by the Karaite Sahal ben Mazzli'ah at the end of the 10th century.)

The most famous Fatimid ruler, the Caliph Al-Hakim (996—1021), was a fanatic who destroyed synagogues and churches, banished the priests and emptied Jerusalem of Jews. Eventually he rescinded some of these restrictions.

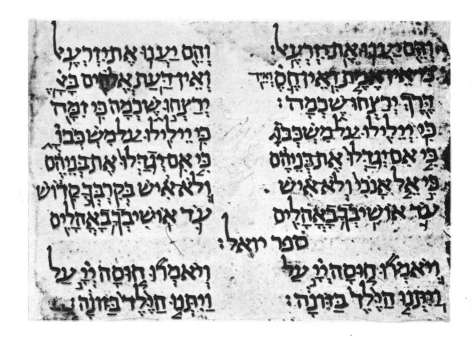

11th CENTURY

The Jewish academy (Yeshiva) of Jerusalem was compelled by the harsh measures of the Caliph Al-Hakim to reestablish itself in Ramla, thirty miles away. Entry to Jerusalem was revived by the "Mourners of Zion", Diaspora Jews who did not cease to lament the destruction of the Temple. This movement which held that *aliyah* — ascent to the Land — would hasten the resurrection of Israel was at its peak in the 9th–11th centuries.

In 1047, the Persian traveller, Nasir-i-Khusraw, related:

"From Byzantium many Christians and Jews come to Jerusalem in order to visit the church and the synagogue there."
(*Book of Travels*, p. 20.)

Large numbers of immigrants and pilgrims also came from Iraq, building synagogues to correspond with their places of origin, such as those in Ramla and Tiberias. The Eretz-Israeli synagogue in Ramla was so defined to distinguish it from the Iraqi one. In 1033 the Jews abandoned the town as

A document from the Cairo Genizah, now at the Freer Gallery of Art, Washington, dating from 1067 CE. It was written by a Jew from Katia, an oasis in northern Sinai, to the Cairo community, and mentions the caravan trade between Syria and Egypt, involving the passage of such products as soap, almonds, etc. The writer reports that many men have moved away fearing that a levy would be imposed on their work. Mention is also made of clashes between Jews and Moslems. The community at Katia still existed in the 15th century together with other communities in northern Sinai, one of them being El-Arish.

35

the result of an earthquake, though they returned some time later. With the approach of the Crusaders, however, many Jews left for Ashkelon, which was fortified.

In 1071, when the Seljuks conquered Jerusalem, the Great Yeshiva moved away to Tyre. The Crusader invasion at the end of the century led to the expulsion of the Jews from Hebron and also marked the end of the Jewish community in Haifa. Several chronicles relate the acts of heroism which the Jews of Haifa had been roused to perform. Marcel Ladoire, a French priest and historian who visited Eretz Israel in 1719, wrote:

"And Haifa, although moderate in size, was strongly fortified, and, perhaps because of this, for a long time it withstood the mighty onslaught of the Prince Tancred, who attacked it from the sea and also from the land, with the help of the Vene-

1.

2. 3.

1. *This scroll, now in Cambridge, is one of the many documents discovered in the archives (Genizah) of a synagogue in Cairo. The scroll laments the destruction of Jewish communities, such as those of Hebron, Ono, Lydda, Jaffa, Hoseifa and Haifa. It is still not clear to which destruction the scroll refers. Some scholars claim that it reflects the conquest of the country by the First Crusade (1099), while others maintain that it refers to the long series of disturbances during the last decades of the early Arab period.*

2. *A letter written by a Jewish scholar in the early part of the 11th century. The writer, Abraham, styling himself "Chief Judge", was captured and ultimately ransomed. He appeals for support to the rich community of Fustat (Old Cairo).*
[J. Mann – Texts and Studies I 352–4]

3. *This fragment was written during the Seljuk invasion of 1071. The writer, Ali Hakohen b. Ezekiel, was in dire straits in Jerusalem and wrote to the heads of the Jewish community of Fustat hoping to receive some aid from them.*
[J. Mann – Texts and Studies I 349–52]

1.

2.

284 VOYAGE

Caïpha n'est aujourd'hui qu'un village habité par des Mahometans, par des Juifs & des Grecs : les ruines des murailles & du château donnent lieu de croire que, quoiqu'elle fût d'une grandeur médiocre, elle étoit tres forte; il falloit qu'elle le fût, puisqu'elle soûtint long-tems contre les vigoureux efforts du Prince Tancrede, quand il l'assiegea par mer & par terre, assisté dans cette expedition par les Venitiens : les Juifs qui la défendoient avec plus de fureur que de courage, furent cependant contraits de ceder à la valeur extraordinaire des assiegeants lorsque les Chrétiens se furent ainsi rendus les maîtres de cette place, ils s'en servirent utilement, son port servant de retraite ordinaire à leurs vaisseaux & à leurs galeres. Ce fut Saladin qui la reprit sur nos

DE LA TERRE SAINTE. 283

Chrétiens, & qui la mit dans l'état qu'on la voit aujourd'hui.

Quand on n'auroit jamais entendu parler de la beauté, de la magnificence & des richesses de la ville de saint Jean d'Acre; à voir seulement les ruines, son port & sa situation, l'on en pourroit juger; son port est tres spacieux, il est dans un golfe, le fond de ce golfe est rond, à l'entrée de ce port est la douanne & une Mosquée; on y trouve encore plusieurs colomnes de marbre de toutes couleurs, dont la plûpart sont brisées; les pieces qui en restent font juger de leur beauté : l'Eglise de saint André étoit sur une éminence proche de la mer, du côté de l'Occident; on voit par ce qui en reste qu'elle ne cedoit en rien aux plus belles Eglises de France; plus de la moitié des piliers & de la voûte de

tians. Although the Jews fought with courage, they were overcome by the might of the invaders."

(M. Ladoire, *Voyage fait à la Terre Sainte en l'année MLCCXIX*, p. 282.)

The well-known historian of the early Crusades, Albert of Aachen, in his *Book of Travels*, refers to the conquest of Haifa by the Crusaders:

"And the city of Haifa . . . which the Jews defended with great courage, to the shame and embarrassment of the Christians."

Jewish communities along the coast, such as those at Rafah, Gaza, Ashkelon, Jaffa and Caesarea, flourished during this century and maintained cultural relations with Egypt. A man from Rafah, living in Egypt, wrote a letter home to the Rafah Jewish community in 1015. It was discovered in the Cairo Genizah. It begins:

"To our beloved Rabbi Solomon, the Judge, may his soul rest in peace, and the elders and the rest of the holy community who dwell in Rafah, may God preserve them."

1. A page from the book, "Travels in the Holy Land", written by the French priest Marcel Ladoire, who visited the country in 1719. The book, published in Paris in 1720, contains a description of Haifa, which was then a small village where the remains of a great Crusader castle were visible. The description is important because it connects these ruins with a traditional account of Jewish heroism in defending Haifa against the Crusaders ·in 1099 CE. Ladoire reports that the efforts made by Prince Tancred and his Venetian army were ineffective against the Jewish defence of the town wall.

2. Among the fragments of the Cairo Genizah is this poem which describes the cruel destruction of the Jewish coastal communities by the Seljuks. The towns of Tyre, Acre and Ashkelon are mentioned. This poem dates to the second half of the 11th century.

The Crusader period can be divided into two distinct phases. The first, lasting until about 1110, was a time of military conquest, during which the Jews suffered considerably and many were slaughtered. In the second phase, the Crusaders gained a hold over certain towns and regions by means of treaties and agreements in which the Jews participated. The destruction of entire communities ceased as the Crusaders were more interested in possessing living cities than in occupying desolate wastes. Jews, however, sought refuge in Ashkelon, Rafah and El Arish ahead of the advancing Crusaders. In more remote areas such as Galilee, the invasion was felt less. Everywhere the Jews were treated by the Crusaders as were other non-Christian communities, except that they were not allowed to live in Jerusalem.

As a result of the Crusades, the Middle East became more closely linked to Europe, thus making travel easier between the two regions. Among the Jews visiting the 'Latin Kingdom of Jerusalem' (Regnum Hierusalem), we can count R. Benjamin of Tudela (visiting between 1167 and 1169), R. Petahia of Regensburg (between 1170 and 1180) and others. The number of Jews immigrating from France, England and North Africa increased.

Despite the Crusader orders banning Jews from settling in Jerusalem, R. Benjamin of Tudela found Jews living near David's Tower. He also noted the existence of Jewish communities in Acre, Tiberias, Caesarea,

Frontispiece of the book describing the travels of Rabbi Benjamin, the son of Jonah, of Tudela, Spain. He travelled through many countries between the years 1165 and 1173, visiting the Holy Land in 1167. The map with a list showing the towns where he found Jews living is given on p. 40. The illustration shown here is from the second edition of his book, which was published in Ferrara, in 1556. The first edition was published in Constantinople in 1543.

מסעות של רבי בנימן ז"ל

אשר הלך בד' ארצות

הנמצאות אל אפסי תבל כאשר יסופר:

נדפס פה פירדא העיר הגדולה והמפוארת

בבית כל אברהם ן' אושקי יע"ו

סנת שי"ו נדפס

Jaffa, Ramla, Ashkelon and Hebron. R. Petahia of Regensburg mentions communities of Jews living in Acre and Tiberias.

Apart from the urban communities there were also rural ones, mainly in Galilee. R. Benjamin of Tudela found Jews in Gush Halav, Kfar Bar'am, 'Amka, Kfar Hannanya, Meron, Dalton and Biriyya.

In 1153, Ashkelon, the last stronghold of the Fatimids in Eretz Israel, fell into the hands of the Crusaders, although the Jewish community continued to exist during the Christian occupation of the town. Benjamin of Tudela found about 200 Rabbinite Jews there as well as 40 Karaites and 300 Samaritans.

In 1187, the Crusaders were defeated by Saladin. Islam once more became the dominant force in the Land and the Jews again enjoyed a certain measure of freedom. The Jewish community in Jerusalem grew considerably after the conquest of Ashkelon by Saladin in 1191. The city was destroyed and many Jews fled the Ayyubids to Jerusalem.

The concept of a messianic movement in Jewish history is a continuous one. The movement expressed the hope for a leader of the House of David and a new political existence for the Jewish people, redeeming the Jews and carrying them back to the Land of Israel.

1.

2.

1. *The Tomb of the Rambam (Maimonides) in Tiberias. He arrived in Eretz Israel with his family in 1165 and settled in Acre. However, because of the disturbances due to the Crusader invasions, he left the country and settled in Egypt, where many of his most important works were written. He eventually became Saladin's court physician. He died in Egypt and, at his request, was buried in Tiberias. This engendered disputes between the various Jewish communities then in Eretz Israel as each wanted him to be buried within its area; his body was eventually brought to Tiberias, where his Tomb has been a centre of pilgrimage for Jews ever since.*

2. *A page of a manuscript of Benjamin of Tudela's travel book. He visited the country in 1167 and saw in Jerusalem "a numerous population composed of Jacobites, Armenians, Greeks, Georgians, Franks, and in fact of all tongues. There's a dyeing house rented yearly by the Jews, exclusively. Two hundred of those Jews dwell in one corner of the city, under the Tower of David."*

In 1127, a scholar named Moses el-Dar'i had announced in Fez, Morocco, the coming of the Messiah.

"He told them that the Messiah was about to appear on the first night of Passover. He advised them to sell all their property. As Passover came and went and nothing happened, these people perished for they had sold all their property and their debts overwhelmed them."
(Maimonides, *Epistle to Yemen,* 103.)

During the first half of the twelfth century (the dates are very confused in the sources mentioning the event) there was a messianic movement led by David Alro'y in the remote eastern districts of the Moslem empire. The apostate to Islam, Samuel al-Maghribi, relates that:

"When the report about him (David Alro'y) reached Baghdad several tidings were spread that he would appoint for them a certain night in which all of them would fly to Jerusalem. The Jews of Baghdad were all led to believe it Their women brought their money and jewels in order that it might be. distributed . . . the men donned green garments and on the night gathered on the roofs expecting to fly to Jerusalem on the wings of angels . . ."
(Samuel al-Maghribi, *Silencing the Jews,* p. 73.)

Around 1172 a Messiah appeared in Yemen. Maimonides, the leader of the Jews in Egypt, advised the Yemenite communities to disregard him or put him to death. In one of his letters he says:

"Many people gathered around him and he was wandering in the mountains. After a year he was caught and all who were with him fled. It was told that there were still many foolish people in Yemen who believed that he would arise and lead them yet."
(Maimonides, in a letter to the scholar of Marseilles, *HUCA* 3, p. 356.)

The famous Jewish traveller, Benjamin of Tudela, who visited the country during the Crusader period, wrote about the Jewish communities in Eretz Israel. The map shown here gives the numbers of the Jewish inhabitants in the various towns in the country. The small numbers undoubtedly reflect the outcome of the destruction of entire communities by the First Crusade, half a century before Benjamin's visit (1167).

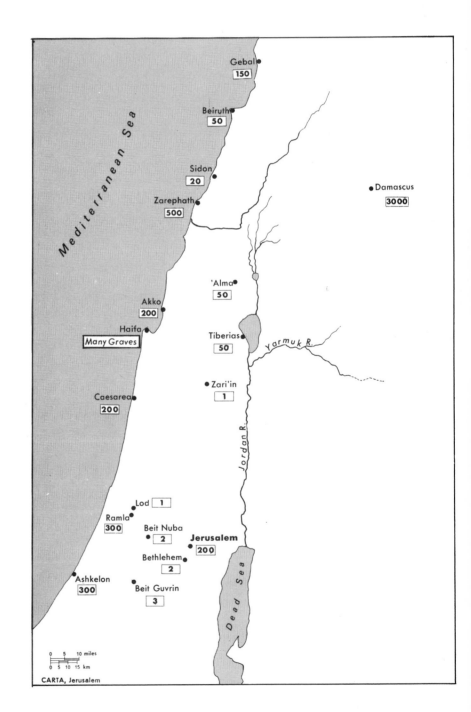

13th CENTURY

In 1211, three hundred Rabbis from France and England immigrated in a group. Some settled in Acre, others in Jerusalem.

After the Mamluks came to power in Egypt and in Syria in 1250, the Jews re-established their old communities. Rabbi Moshe ben Nahman (Nahmanides), a famous physician and outstanding talmudic scholar (1194–1270), went from Spain to the Mamlakat al-Sham (region of Syria), as it was called by the Mamluks. At first he settled in Jerusalem (all the districts from Gaza in the south to Aleppo in the north were considered Syrian territory) where he used an old deserted house as a synagogue, bringing the Scrolls of Law from Nablus whither they had been sent for safekeeping. Then he moved to Acre and here he engaged in disseminating Jewish teaching among the local population. Many of the immigrants who came during this century, especially those who had been expelled from France, were highly educated. They settled mainly in the coastal cities of Haifa, Caesarea,

The Arab geographer Dimashqi, who wrote (1300) about the wonders of nature, included in his treatise a paragraph describing the ceremonies being held at Meron, in northern Galilee. In Meron, he thus relates: "there is a cave, dry all through the year except on one day when the Jews gather together from near and far, to pray. Then suddenly, water flows for two hours, then it stops." Obviously Jewish communities existed in Galilee at the end of the 13th century, despite the Mongol invaders who destroyed towns throughout the country.

شـبـاط وجمع له ما بعده عليهنّ في الماء من زبد نظهر من أنواههنّ في تلك المدّة على وجه الماء وبكنّ زوجين زوجين متراكبات ثمّ أكل من تلك الرغوة المزبدة بسـيرا أعظم إنعاظا شـديـدا لا يفتر حتّى يصبّ عليه الماء البارد ولو ما عسى أن يدوم لا ينفكّ منعطا (a وكذلك يفعل أكله من ذلك السمك والإناث منه للإناث والذكور منه للذكور والله عزّ وجلّ أعلم بذلك b، قال صاحب نحفة الغرائب بين خلاط وأرزن عين تسّى جرة بغور الماء منها فورا شديدا ويسمع هديره من بعد ويسبع بسرا ثمّ يغور في الأرض ومن شرب منها مات في وقته وساعته وبرى حولها جثّ طير ووحش ما شاء الله وبالقرب أناس يعرسون الناس المارّين لئلّا يشربوا منها وهى تغور من الأرض ثمّ تغور بالقرب منها ولا ينبت حولها نبات b، وبجبل الزابود (b من أرض صغر قرية يقال لها ميرون وفيها مغارة فيها نواويس وأحواض لا تزال طول السنة بابسـة ليس فيها قطرة الماء ولا نداوة ولا رشّح أصلا فإذا كان يوم من السنة آجتمع إليها ناس من اليهود من البلاد البعيدة والقريبة والفلّاحين، وغيرهم وأقاموا طول نهارهم بدخلون إليها ويخرجون منها وهى بجالها من البياس ثمّ ما يشعرون إلّا والماء دافق من تلك الأحواض والنواويس وساح على الأرض في المغارة مقدار ساعة أو ساعتين ثمّ ينقطع وهذا يوم عيد اليهود ويعملون ذلك الماء إلى البلاد البعيدة والقريبة في البرّ والبحر ويقال هذا ماء ميرون b، وبالقرب من ميرون واد بينها وبين صغد واد يقال له وادى دليبه (c فيه عين تغور من الأرض يقعد عندها الناس بغسلون عليها ويشربون من مائها ساعة وساعتين ثمّ إنّ العين تنقطع كأن لم يكن فيها ماء وهى تخرج من وجه الأرض فيقول الناس الحاضرون. يا شيخ مسعود عطشنا يخرج الماء في الوادى إلى الطواحين ثمّ ينقطع وينشف كأن لم يكن ثمّ يبعدون القول فتخرج العين ثمّ ينشف ثمّ يبعدون القول فتجرى وهذا القول دأبها دائما على ممرّ السنين والأوقات b، وبالماغوصة من جزيرة قبرس صخرة فيها نقير يسع عشرة أرطال بالدمشقى مائها وبالقرب من الصخرة بئر فيه ماء يستقى منه ما بلاء ذلك النقير ويغطّى أبّاما فيكون زاجا أصغر من أجود أنواع الزاج وهو الزاج القبرصيّ الخالص وهذا النقير في دار قوم بتوارثونها

a) St.-Pét. et L. om. les mots depuis وكذلك jusqu'à la fin de la phrase. b) St.-Pét. et L. الرابود. c) Peut-être faut-il lire دليبه.

41

Tyre and Acre, but were forced to re-settle inland later on as a result of the Mamluk 'scorched earth' policy of destroying these cities in order to prevent a new Crusader invasion.

The wealthiest Jewish community during this century was that of Acre, which had benefitted from various waves of immigration. In 1257, R. Yehiel of Paris settled there and established the 'Yeshiva of Paris'. The community was totally destroyed with the fall of Acre in 1291 when it was conquered by the Mamluk sultan Al-Ashraf Khalil, son of Qalawun.

The Jewish communities of Galilee continued to preserve their traditions. There was a synagogue in Safad. R. Yehiel of Paris describes the custom of making a pilgrimage to Meron:

". . . and there the Israelites and the Arabs assembled on the festival of Pesach Sheni to pray and sing their

1.

كرّه بكسر اوله وفتح ثانيه مدينة بساجستان كذا يقوله العجم ويكتب بالجيم جرّه وقد ذكرناه فى بابه ٤

كرزنة هو فيما احسب موضع فى جزيرة الاندلس فى فحص البلّوط ينسب اليه المنذر بن سعيد البلوطى القاضى وايضا القاضى ابو عبد الله محمد بن احمد بن خلف الكرزى القرطبى يروى عن اى المطرف عبد الرحمن بن القاسم بن محمد الشعبى المالقى روى عنه السلفى بالاجازة وقل تنسل فى جامع قرطبة سنة ٨٩ او سنة ثمان فى يوم جمعة بغير حقّ ٤

كبريزيم بيت عبادة للسامرة بن اليهود بنابلس يزعمون ان الذبح فيه كن ٥اوان الذبيح هو اسحاق والسامرة والسامرة بن اليهود بنابلس كثيرون لذلك ٥

باب الكاف والسين وما يليهما

كساب بالصم واخره باء موحدة موضع فى قول عمر بن ربيعه حتى المنازل قد عمرن خرايا بين الجرير وبين ركن كسابا فانتقى من ملكن غير رنّمها مرّ السحاب المعقبات سكابا دار الله قلبى غداة لقيتها عند الجزار فا عيينه جوابا

1. A page from the geographical dictionary written by Yaqut (d. 1229) in which he defines Gerizim as a "place of worship of the Samaritans from among the Jews", in Shechem (Nablus).

2. A view of the walls of Acre. This town formed the main harbour of Israel in mediaeval times and also became one of the most important centres of the Jews in the country. In the 12th century it served as the scene of a religious dispute with Maimonides, indicating the existence of a centre of learning there. In the 13th century the Ramban (Nahmanides) landed in the Holy Land at this harbour. He also died there. According to an old tradition, Acre was a Gentile town and therefore had no cemetery, its Jews being buried in Haifa or Kfar Yasif, east of Acre. Yet the local community was always an important one. In the 18th century Haim Farhi, a Jew, organised the successful defence of Acre and Western Galilee against the siege of Napoleon. Many Jewish scholars and writers have lived there.

2.

litanies . . . and often there is no water there, and while they are praying the water flows immediately."

Contemporary Arab authors, such as Dimashqi, who in 1300 wrote a book about natural phenomena, provided evidence of the custom of making a pilgrimage to the grave of R. Shimon bar Yohai in Meron.

"And at Mount Zabud in the Safad region there is a village called Meron where there is a cave which contains caverns and sources of water which are dry throughout the entire year, without a drop of water. And on a fixed day each year groups of Jews from the surrounding region and distant villages gather there together and spend the day there. They enter the cave and do not leave it and it is dry until suddenly, imperceptibly, the water flows into the caverns and wells up, flooding the floor of the cave for an hour or two and then it ceases. This is a feast day for the Jews; they take this water to many places, both near and far, on land and across the sea, calling it 'Meron Water.' "
(From a book written by Dimashqi at the end of the 13th century, *Knowledge of Wonders at Sea and on Land*, p. 118.)

1.

1. Nahmanides' Seal
The seal was discovered early in 1972 on the ground at a distance of about 100 metres east of Tel Kisan, in the Valley of Acre. The seal is round and made of cast copper; its diameter is 21.6 × 22.3 mm., its height, including the handle — 17 mm.; produced by the arachnoid casting method — "cire perdue". The writing on the seal is a classic example of Spanish-Hebrew, similar to Hebrew inscriptions of the 13th and 14th centuries, discovered in the district of Nahmanides' birth and activity in Spain. Nahmanides came to Eretz Israel in 1267, staying in Jerusalem at least until after the Day of Atonement of the year 5028, but in that very year he returned to Acre — home of the largest and most important Jewish community in the Holy Land in the 13th century.

2

2. The Ramban synagogue in Jerusalem. This synagogue is mentioned in a letter written by Nahmanides to his son in Spain, in 1267, where he reports the conversion of a ruin into a synagogue. This is probably the oldest synagogue in Jerusalem still in use. In his letter Nahmanides writes that the ruin had marble columns and a dome. For the consecration of the synagogue he sent an emissary to Shechem (Nablus) to bring a scroll of the law (sefer torah) from there. After the Ottoman conquest (1517) the building was appropriated by the Arabs and had been used as a cheesemakers' shop until recently.

14th CENTURY

The Mamluks, originally slave-soldiers in Egypt who had rebelled against the former Ayyubid sultans in 1250 and continued to rule until 1517, had governed not only Egypt but Syria (including the Land of Israel) as well. Their rule restored calm to the country and permitted renewed Jewish settlement. Ashtory Ha-Parhi, a Jewish geographer from Florenca, Spain, after a brief stay in Jerusalem settled in Beth She'an, where there seems to have been a Jewish community. In 1322, he wrote his famous book on the topography of Eretz Israel, *Kaftor Veferach.* Other Jewish communities existed at this time in Safad, Ramla and Gaza. Natural disasters, such as epidemics and earthquakes, hindered the renaissance of Jewish life in the country during this century.

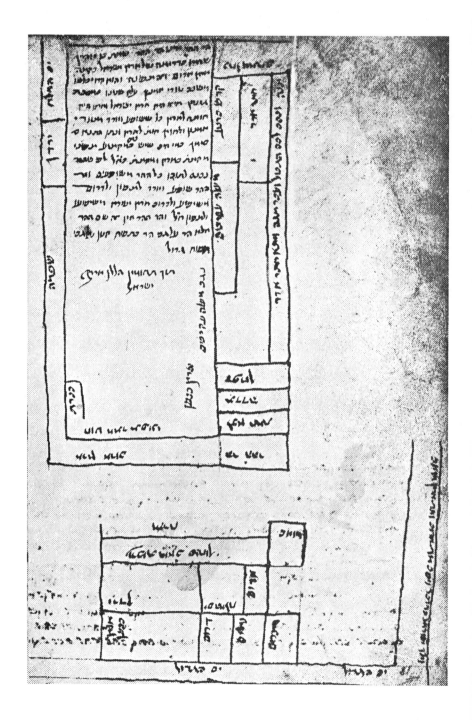

This manuscript, kept in the British Museum, is a Hebrew map of Eretz Israel in the 14th century, showing the country schematically. The borders and some cities are described according to biblical or other literary sources. The map faces south and lists such places as Cana'an, the Dead Sea and the River Jordan. The lower part shows Palestine in relation to neighbouring countries.

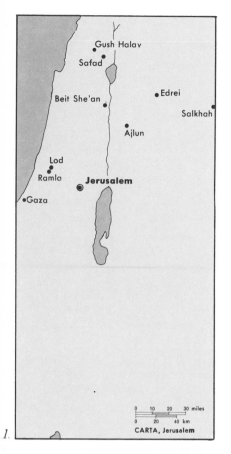

In his book, *Liber Peregrinationis*, Jacques of Verona, an Augustine monk who visited the country in 1335, notes that there was a long-established Jewish community at the foot of Mount Zion in the area known as the Jewish Quarter. He also refers to the local Jews who helped him in touring the country.

"A pilgrim who wished to visit ancient forts and towns in the Holy Land would have been unable to locate these without a good guide who knew the Land well or without one of the Jews who lived there. The Jews were able to recount the history of these places since this knowledge had been handed down from their forefathers and wise men. So when I journeyed overseas I often requested and managed to obtain an excellent guide among the Jews who lived there."
(Jacques of Verona, *Liber Peregrinationis*, p. 65.)

Another traveller, Ogier D'Anglure (visiting in 1395), mentions in his book, *Le Saint Voyage de Jérusalem*, that the Jews in the Holy City had their own special residential areas.

During the middle of the century, a

LE

SAINT VOYAGE

DE

JHERUSALEM

DU SEIGNEUR D'ANGLURE

PUBLIE PAR

FRANÇOIS BONNARDOT & AUGUSTE LONGNON

PARIS

LIBRAIRIE DE FIRMIN DIDOT ET Cⁱᵉ

56, RUE JACOB, 56

M DCCC LXXVIII

1. This map shows towns in Eretz Israel where Jewish communities existed in the 14th century. The places are mentioned by Ashtory Ha-Parhi, but there is no doubt that there were many more.

2. The title page of the book "Kaftor Veferach", the first modern Hebrew-Jewish book on the geography of Palestine. It was printed in Venice in 1549, although it was written in 1322. The author, Ashtory Ha-Parhi, immigrated from Spain. At first he settled in Jerusalem but later moved to Beth She'an. He used to travel throughout the country extensively and would then record the details of what he had observed. He tried to identify biblical sites and connect them with existing places.

3. The cover of the book mentioned in the text.

Yeshiva, "Assir Hatiqva", was established in Jerusalem, the head of which was R. Isaac Halevi.

Giorgio Gucci, a Florentine pilgrim visiting the Holy Places in 1384, relates that in Gaza, too, as in Jerusalem, the Jews preferred to live separately. Christian travellers such as Gucci and Ludoph von Suchem, who wrote his book in 1350, tell about the Jews of the southern region of the country coming to the Cave of Machpelah to pray. Thus writes Ludoph von Suchem:

"Going on from Beersheba one comes to a fair and ancient city named Hebron. On the side of a hill near this city there stands a fair church, wherein is the double cave wherein the three patriarchs, Abraham, Isaac and Jacob, are buried together with their wives. This church is held especially sacred by the Saracens. They suffer Jews to enter, which in my time they paid money to do."

Jews began to move from the villages of Galilee to the urban community of Safad, also designated the administrative capital of the region. Documents by contemporary authors register the complaints made by Moslem residents of Safad about extensive Jewish building there.

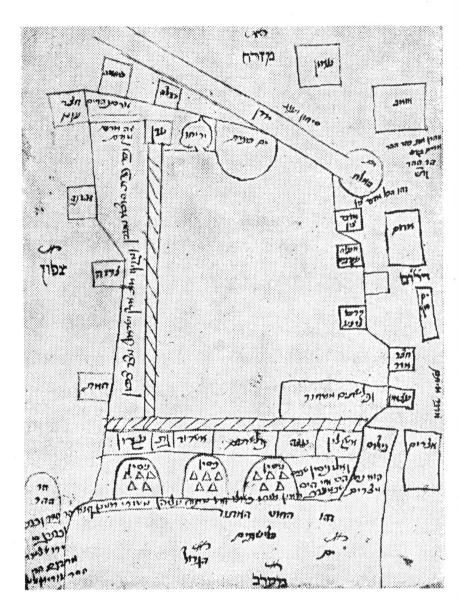

1. *A Hebrew map, now kept in the British Museum, shows Eretz Israel, probably during the 15th—16th centuries. Along the sea coast, at the bottom of the map, such cities as Ashkelon, Gaza, Ashdod, Gath and Ekron are mentioned. The islands (probably those of Greece) are marked in the sea. In the south the Nile is named as well as some of the stations of the Exodus, including Jericho (at the top). The River Jordan flows from the Sea of Galilee down to the Dead Sea.*

2. *Inscription: "Rabbi Jeremiah, the son of Guedalia, the son of Rabbi Joseph." On one of the stones of the southern wall of the Temple area in Jerusalem, placed there by a Jewish pilgrim in the Middle Ages.*

15th CENTURY

At the beginning of the 15th century the immigration of Jews from European countries increased. Attempts by the German Jews to acquire the room above the Tomb of David at Mount Zion had serious results. The Latin friars (Franciscans) had established a monastery on Mount Zion in 1354 and since then the possession of sites in this place became a source of disputes. When in 1428 Jews tried to purchase rooms and buildings on Mount Zion, the Christians applied to the Pope, who asked the Italian merchant republics to stop taking Jews on board their ships sailing to the Holy Land. The Mamluk government also harassed the Jews in Jerusalem, and in about 1440 it imposed a heavy tax on them to be paid yearly. Most Jews were craftsmen or small merchants who could not afford to pay the tax. Many of them left Jerusalem.

Two 15th-century etchings. The upper one shows a Jewish money-changer in Jerusalem with a client. The lower one shows Jerusalem Jews and Moslems at a celebration. The etchings are from a book written by Bernhard von Breidenbach, who visited Palestine in 1483, travelling throughout the country. He was of an aristocratic German family and his last post was that of Dean of Mainz Cathedral. His book was published, in Latin, in 1486. He writes about Jews in Hebron and Jerusalem, noting that Hebrew was their language, and also says: "They (the Jews) will treat you (the travellers) in full fidelity — more so than anyone else in those countries of the unbelievers."

In 1438, an Italian rabbi, Elijah of Ferrara, settled in Jerusalem and became the spiritual head of the community.

In 1470, R. Isaac b. Meir Latif counted 150 Jewish families in Jerusalem, a number which rose by the end of the century.

In 1474, the Moslems destroyed an old synagogue, and the Jews had to bribe the authorities to allow them to erect a new one on the ruins. This is reported by Mujir al-Din, the outstanding historian of Jerusalem in this century (d. 1521). He also relates that the Jews of Jerusalem lived in the Street of the Jews and the gate then standing slightly east of the present Zion Gate was called the Gate of the Jewish Quarter.

With the coming of R. Ovadiah of Bertinoro, in 1488, the state of the Jewish community was changed. R. Ovadiah, a famous Mishnah commentator, became the spiritual leader of Jerusalem Jewry, and during the period of his rabbinate he succeeded in uniting the oppressed and divided community. He found in Jerusalem no more than 70 Jewish families and many widows. Soon afterwards, the government abolished the heavy tax and the Italian republics once more allowed Jews to travel in their ships to the Land of Israel. At this time the immigration of the Spanish exiles began. A pupil of R. Ovadiah relates in a letter written in 1495 that about 200 Jewish families were living in Jerusalem.

The famous chronicler of Jerusalem in the Mamluk period, Mujir al-Din (who wrote his book in 1496), gives the detailed story of the Jewish synagogue which was taken by force, in 1473, by the Moslem authorities. The building was very badly damaged by weathering and by local fanatics but at last it was reopened as a synagogue, after the intervention of the Mamluk sultan. The synagogue was identified as that of the Ramban (Nahmanides), which is located in the main street of the Jewish Quarter in the Old City of Jerusalem.

عليه السلام وجلسوا ومعهم أكابر بلد الخليل وكتبوا محاضر بما وقع من
النهب والقتل والسبى فى ذلك ثم قبض الحاصكى على أكابر بلد الخليل
من القضاة والمشايخ وطلب منهم اثنى عشر ألف دينار وتوجه وهم معه
معتقلا عليهم الى ان وصل الى مدينة غزة فقتله بشبك العلائى نائب غزة
بمرسوم شريف ورد عليه من السلطان خفية وأشاع انه دخل الى
الاصطبل ليأخذ فرساً طلبها من النائب فوقع عليه حائط فات وكان
موته فى يوم الاربعاء حادى عشر رجب وثارت فتنة بسببه بالقاهرة من
المماليك الجلبان واعتذرهم السلطان وأنكر أن يكون أمر نائب
غزة بقتله وحلف على ذلك ومما وقع انه لما ضرب الشيخ زين الدين عبد
القادر بن قطلوشاه كما تقدم وكان من أهل القرآن وضرب بغير حق وكان
يتضرع الى الله ويدعو عليه فبينما هو ذات ليلة نائم فى فراشه والى جانبه
زوجته وهى ابنة عمه اذ سمعته وهو نائم يقول اللهم خلص حقى عاجلا فانى
لا أصبر الى الآخرة لا أصبر الى الآخرة كررها ثلاثا
ثم استيقظ من نومه فأخبرته زوجته بما سمعت منه فصدقها على انه تكلم
بذلك فى رؤيا وآراها فى صبيحة تلك الليلة ورد الخبر الى القدس بهلاك
بغزة فسبحان قاصم الجبارة ثم توجه أهل الخليل الى حضرة السلطان ولم
يحصل لهم الا الخير ببركة سيدنا الخليل عليه الصلاة والسلام وعادوا الى
أوطانهم وتراجع أمر مدينة الخليل الى العمارة وصلح حالها والله الحمد
(واقعة كنيسة اليهود) وفيها وقعت حادثة بالقدس الشريف وهى
ان بحارة اليهود مسجدا للمسلمين عليه منارة وهو بأصق كنيسة اليهود ومن
جهة القبلة ويتوصل الى المسجد من زقاق مستطيل من جهة القبلة
وبجوار المسجد من جهة الغرب دار من جملة أوقاف اليهود فوقع المطر
فى زمن الشتاء ولعله فى شهر جمادى الآخرة فهدمت الدار المذكورة
فكشف باب المسجد من جهة الشارع المسلوك فقصد المسلمون
الاستيلاء على الدار المنهدمة وأن يكون الاستطراق الى المسجد منها

1.

Die Pilgerfahrt

des

Ritters Arnold von Harff

von

Cöln durch Italien, Syrien, Aegypten, Arabien, Aethiopien, Nubien, Palästina, die Türkei, Frankreich und Spanien,

wie er sie

in den Jahren 1496 bis 1499

vollendet,

beschrieben und durch Zeichnungen erläutert hat.

Nach den ältesten Handschriften

und mit deren 47 Bildern in Holzschnitt

herausgegeben von

Dr. E. von GROOTE.

Cöln 1860.

Verlag von J. M. Heberle (H. Lempertz).

Steven's Druckerei, Köln, Brüderstr. 14.

2.

Meshullam of Volterra, who visited the Land of Israel in 1481, tells of Jewish house- and property-owners in Gaza, Hebron and Jerusalem.

A famous traveller of this period, the Dominican monk Felix Fabri, who visited the country twice (in 1480 and in 1484), relates in his *Evagatorium in Terram Sanctam* that there were Jews in Jerusalem and Gaza.

A Christian pilgrim from Bohemia (visiting in 1491–1492), Martin Kabtanik, wrote in his book *Journey to Jerusalem*:

"Christians and Jews alike in Jerusalem lived in great poverty and in conditions of great deprivation, there are not many Christians but there are many Jews, and these the Moslems persecute in various ways. Christians and Jews go about in Jerusalem in clothes considered fit only for wandering beggars. The Moslems know that the Jews think and even say that this is the Holy Land which has been promised to them and that those Jews who dwell there are regarded as holy by Jews elsewhere, because, in spite of all the troubles and sorrows inflicted on them by the Moslems, they refuse to leave the Land."

Arnold von Harff, a Christian traveller from Germany, wrote in the account of his journey, made in 1497–1498,

"In Jerusalem dwell many Jews, amongst them learned rabbis; others, who were born in Lombardy, are well-versed in the Christian Testament, and I found also three German Jews in Jerusalem."

1. *Mujir al-Din names in his book the gates of the Old City. Concerning Zion Gate, in the southern part of the town, he adds that it was known by the name "Gate of the Jewish Quarter" (Bab harat al-yahud).*

2. *The cover of the book mentioned in the text.*

16th CENTURY

In 1517, the country was conquered by the Ottoman Turks, whose regime was to last exactly four hundred years. Throughout this period there were four centres of Jewish life: Jerusalem, Safad, Tiberias and Hebron.

The largest community, numbering about 10,000 Jews, was situated in and around Safad; most of them were refugees from Spain, from which they were expelled in 1492. The Jews of Safad were reported as trading in spices, cheese, oil, vegetables, and fruits. Many Jews were engaged in weaving. Among the prominent leaders of the community in the 16th century was R. Jacob Berav, who tried to renew rabbinical ordination (*semikhah*). Other prominent rabbis included R. Joseph Karo, compiler of the 'Shulhan Arukh'. The Cabbalist R. Isaac Luria and his important disciple R. Hayyim Vital resided there for some time. During this century Safad was the centre of Jewish mysticism.

In 1586 the authorities finally deprived the Jerusalem community of the synagogue named after Nahmanides.

Although the Jews lost central places of worship, they held on to the site of the Tomb of Samuel, on the highest mountain overlooking Jerusalem from the north. Pantales de Aveiro, a Portuguese Christian traveller, visited the Holy Land in 1560. He reports that Jews went to the grave every eight days to light candles. In his *Itinerario de Terra Sancta* we read:

The Istanbuli synagogue in the Jewish Quarter of Jerusalem. It forms part of the group of four Sephardi synagogues built by newcomers from Spain in the 16th century. The name of the synagogue indicates that its founders came from Spain via Istanbul, where they were made welcome, but soon went on to Jerusalem.

"St. Samuel (i.e., Samuel the prophet, whose traditional burial place became a shrine for the three major religions). This is the only place which the Jews who live in the Holy Land maintain by themselves."

Joseph Nasi, the Jewish statesman, born in Portugal at the beginning of the 16th century, served in the court of the Turkish Sultan Sulayman. There he obtained permission for the Jews to settle in Tiberias, and in seven adjoining villages.

According to official censuses in the second quarter of the century, the number of Jews in Jerusalem varied between approximately 1,000 and 1,500. They lived in three quarters, co-terminous with the Jewish Quarter of our time.

Waldrich Pefat, a traveller from Wilkanau who visited the Holy Land between 1546 and 1547, wrote:

"Many Jews dwell in Jerusalem, and there is a special street of the Jews."

1—2. When the Jews were expelled from Spain in 1492 many found their way to the Turkish empire, where they succeeded in attaining high positions. Their influence helped many Spanish Jews to settle in Jerusalem after 1516. The newcomers built a new synagogue, named Eliyahu Hanavi, and soon afterwards three more synagogues were built. The group of four synagogues still exists (though used as a garbage dump during the Jordanian occupation of 1948—67), and is once again restored. The photograph to the left shows the double arch of "Ben Zakkai", while that on the right shows the "bima" (dais) of the "Istanbuli" synagogue.

3. Ha'ari (Ashkenazi) synagogue in Safad. It was built at the end of the 16th century and is dedicated to Ha'ari (Rabbi Isaac Luria, 1534—1573), founder of a mystical movement which lasted for several centuries, centred in Safad. The synagogue was constructed on the spot where it was believed that Ha'ari and his disciples used to greet the Sabbath.

William Biddulph, an English priest who visited the country in 1600 together with a group of English pilgrims, remarks in his book *The Travels of Four Englishmen and a Preacher*:

"Tiberias, the town that Salim gave to Graziola (Dona Grazia, mother-in-law of Joseph the President, that is, Joseph Nasi) a Jewish grande dame, is entirely occupied by Jews."

For the rural communities of Jews in this century we have the testimony of Pierre Belon, a French doctor from Mans, who travelled in Galilee in 1547. He wrote:

"We look around Lake Tiberias and see the villages of Beth Saida and Korazim. Today Jews are living in these villages and they have built up again all the places around the lake, started fishing industries and have once again made the earth fruitful, where once it was desolate."
(P. Belon, *Les Observations de Plusieurs Singularités et Choses Memorables . . . p. 148—149.*)

1. This book provides further evidence of the great cultural renaissance which occurred in and around Safad. The book called *Seder Hayom* (daily order) was written in Ein Zeitim near Safad by Rabbi Moshe ben Machir, in 1575. It is a kind of commentary on daily prayers. The first edition was printed in Venice in 1599.

2. This document from the 16th century is believed to have been issued by the Turkish Sultan or his Grand Vizier. It is kept in the State Archives in Istanbul. It is a "firman" (decree) dated 1578, to the Qadi (judge) of Safad, and refers to a decree deporting Safad's Jewish population to Cyprus . . . "If it is decided, to deport them to Cyprus, the public revenue will lose money and the town of Safad will be on the verge of ruin." In the end the decree was not enforced.

3. In the 16th century Safad became the major Jewish community in Eretz Israel, one of the most famous inhabitants being Rabbi Joseph Karo, author of the Shulhan Aruch. This book, which soon spread throughout the Jewish world, contains a codification of Jewish law. It was written between the years 1555 and 1563. Shown here is the title page from the first edition, printed in Venice in 1565.

4. Part of a map of illustrations to a book published in Italy in 1598, which describes the visit to Eretz Israel of a Jew from Casale Monferrato in northern Italy. The section reproduced here shows the Cave of Machpelah in Hebron and describes the plight of the Jews who frequent the area but are refused access to the cave by the Arabs.

17th CENTURY

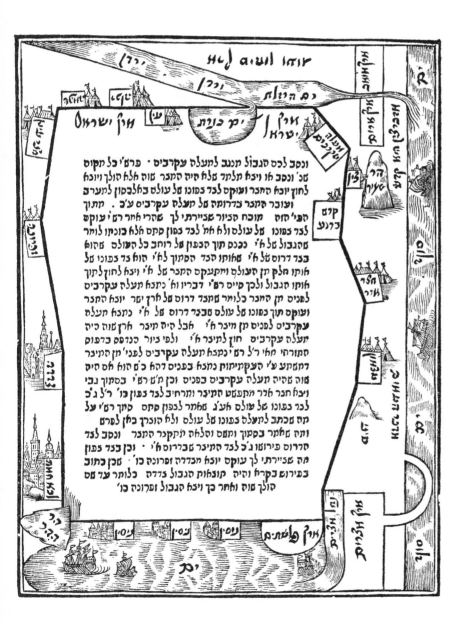

During this century both the activity and the wealth of the Jewish community in the Land declined as a result of the end of the immigration of Jews expelled from Spain. The political, economic and security situation of the country deteriorated as well. Various natural disasters such as epidemics, droughts and locusts decimated the population. The Ottoman rulers became lax, and inefficient and rapacious local administrators (such as Fakhr al-Din II, 1598–1635) usurped authority. Economic conditions worsened, taxes mounted, and general distintegration set in.

A Christian writer, Eugene Roger, records in approximately 1631 that there were 15,000 Jews living in various parts of the country, including Jerusalem, Hebron, Gaza, Haifa, Ramla, Nablus, Safad, Acre and Sidon. The Jews were subject to the whims of the local rulers, who in many cases had purchased their posts at great cost and attempted to recoup this money during their period of rule. Large numbers of Jews left Galilee and went to Jerusalem, leading to a revival of the Jewish community there.

Ignatius von Rheinfelden, a Franciscan monk from Germany who visited the Holy Land in 1656, commented in a book entitled *New Jerusalemite Pilgrimages*:

This map was prepared by R. Mordechai Jaffe in 1603. Based on an earlier map of the year 1523, it shows the wanderings of the Children of Israel from Egypt to the Land of Israel. The map is bounded by the Red Sea on the right, the Mediterranean at the bottom, the Jordan and its lakes at the top and the Syrian border on the left. Marked in squares are the names of various localities, both in Sinai and in the Land of Israel.

"In Jerusalem there also live many Jews who came from all over the world to await the coming of the Messiah and to welcome him... Some Jews who can afford it leave instructions in their wills that after their death their bodies should be transferred to Jerusalem and buried in the Valley of Jehoshaphat."

Jews in Jerusalem earned their living as peddlars, tailors, or cobblers. There are accounts that the important community of Tiberias was abandoned in 1670 because of the ruthlessness of the Turks.

In 1700, the distinguished leader, Rabbi Yehuda the Hassid (Judah the Pious), immigrated from Poland to Eretz Israel, together with a group of his students and their families. This initially had a positive effect on the Jews already living there, but the Jewish community was again left without a leader upon Rabbi Yehuda's death, shortly after he had reached Jerusalem.

1. Two pomegranates and three Torah plates from the Nazi robbery of Jewish communities. These 17th century religious objects, belonging to the community of Nablus, probably were sold in a period of decline during the 19th century to a Jewish community in Europe. The Torah plates are meant to mark which scroll should be read on Sabbath, which scroll should be read on the semi-festival marking the start of the month, and which on holydays.

2. This map shows a number of villages mentioned in official Turkish documents. These documents, giving lists of the inhabitants of the country, were used for taxation purposes. They usually refer to land- and house-owners and consequently do not give an accurate picture of the Jewish population. A Jewish traveller, who visited the same villages at approximately the time that these lists were drawn up, gives different figures for the Jewish population. Nevertheless, they are important as they tell us of the existence of Jewish farmers in the most remote parts of Palestine.

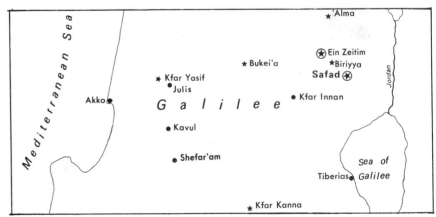

54

1.

2.

Various travellers of this period have provided us with information about Jews living in the country. One of them is George Sandys, son of the Archbishop of York, who visited the Land of Israel in 1611. In his *Travailes* he wrote:

"And in their Land they (the Jews) live as strangers, hated by those amongst whom they dwell, open to all oppression and deprivation, which they bear with patience beyond all belief, despised and beaten. In spite of all this, I never saw a Jew with an angry face."

Antonius Gonsalez, a Spanish Franciscan monk who visited the Holy Land in 1665, wrote:

"There are large numbers of Jews everywhere."

A Dutch scholar, Olf Dapper, collected data on the Holy Land in this period, mostly from travellers who wrote descriptions of their journeys. In 1677 he published a book summing up his research. There we read:

"There are Jews all over Syria and the Holy Land, especially in Acre, Sidon, Damascus, Jerusalem, Hebron and Gaza. No transactions take place without the knowledge of the Jews and even the smallest dealings pass through their hands."

The most famous aspirations of a messianic redemption were expressed in the movement led by Sabbatai Zevi from Smyrna, Turkey, in 1660. His followers fervently believed that their Messiah would achieve a miraculous victory. Instead they were cruelly disappointed when he became a convert to Islam rather than face punishment.

The prime exponent of the Cabbalists, Rabbi Isaac Luria, established Safad as a town of mystic lore in the 16th century. Rabbi Luria was born in Jerusalem in 1534 and died in Safad in 1573. He is known as Ha'ari (the lion). The photographs show both Ha'ari synagogues in Safad which have been in continuous use since then.

55

18th CENTURY

During this century the Ottoman empire and its provinces continued to decay economically and culturally, and local rulers continued to exploit their regions and the population. But the immigration of Jews to the Land of Israel did not cease and, although life became increasingly difficult there, the growing Jewish communities began to organise themselves.

With the renewed impetus of Jewish settlement in Galilee during the first half of this century two events deserve mention. First, the creation in Kefar Yasif of a new Jewish village which engaged in agri-

1.

1. Scroll-case and pomegranates now at Hebrew Union College Museum, Cincinnati. They are made of silver and were found at Shechem (Nablus); they date from the 17th–18th centuries, or possibly earlier. They are fashioned in the style of the Sephardi Jews, who use the case to hold the scroll during the public reading.

2. The doors to the synagogue of Abraham the Patriarch at Hebron which were brought from Gaza in 1835. The doors disappeared during the destruction of the Jewish community of Hebron in the riots of 1929. They were beautifully carved with typical Arab designs in sycamore wood. The synagogue from which they came, in Gaza, was destroyed and its stones were re-used in 1835 to build the citadel in Ashkelon.

2.

1.

2.

culture and also observed the religious laws applicable to the Land of Israel. The community left in 1707 as a result of a plague of locusts, but was restored in 1747, by the Cabbalist R. Solomon Abbadi, who sought, under the protection of Sheikh Dahir al-'Umar, the ruler of Galilee, to establish a Torah centre. Connections of Jewish citizens with the centre led to the restoration of another settlement. R. Hayyim Abulafia, who was born in Hebron but moved to Jerusalem and then to Safad, was appointed Rabbi of Smyrna. From Smyrna he was invited in 1740 by Sheikh Dahir al-'Umar, to

1. Hanukkah lamp, made of silver with brass. Made in Jerusalem in the 18th century.

2. Amulet. Manuscript in black ink on cut parchment of the 18th century. In the shape of a rectangular building topped by a small cupola; symmetric design, cut with a knife; at the top — two upright lions, with open jaws, supporting a shield; at the bottom — a seven-branched candelabrum flanked by deer.

1.

"come up and take possession of the Land which was the Land of your fathers."

This started a new phase in the history of the Jewish community of Tiberias.

The Florentine-Christian pilgrim, Giovanni Mariti, who completed his journeys in the East in 1768, reports in his *Voyages*:

"The Jews also have there (in Acre) a small synagogue which they cannot widen, since the governor demands from them to be content with the piece of earth they possess, which he permits them to have."

Frederick Hasselquist, a Swedish doctor and naturalist who visited the country in 1751, estimates that 4,000 Jews reached the Holy Land that year. In 1777, 300 immigrants settled in Safad, giving added impetus to Jewish settlement in Galilee. The number of synagogues in Safad rose from seven to thirty.

2.

1. The Maran Beth Joseph synagogue in Safad is named after Rabbi Joseph Karo, the compiler of the Shulchan Aruch, the code of religious law for daily Jewish life.

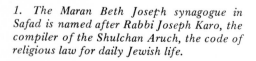

2. Amulet. Silver round, concave disc with aperture for hanging; engraved on one side; tendrillar ornaments.

1.

19thCENTURY

With the increasing impoverishment of the Ottoman empire, the burden of taxation pressed ever more heavily on the inhabitants of Eretz Israel. The Turkish army struggled continually to withstand attacks by Beduin tribes. Villagers were forced to flee to the cities and this, together with various natural disasters, led to a decrease in population. It is estimated that during the first half of this century the population of the country did not exceed 250,000.

William Turner, an English diplomat and writer (1792–1867) who visited the country in 1815, wrote a *Journal* of his tour in which he noted:

"The present population (in Acre) is from 7 to 8,000, of whom the Turks are a third, the Maronites, Roman Catholics and Jews together

2.

1. Dedication sign. 19th century; cut and engraved silver; arched hand with short fingers, its edges adorned with a vegetal design.

2. Sash for Torah scroll: Jerusalem 1873. Woven silk; fringes, ornamental stripes and Shield of David at either end.

3. Wall decoration. 19th century; hewn and painted wood; a wide shield, its frame decorated with vine leaves and clusters of grapes, branches, in the centre a ribbon with inscription: "Thy wife shall be as a fruitful vine" (Psalms 128:3), crowned by a Shield of David.

3.

not above 500 in all, and the remainder Greeks."

In Tiberias, Turner inquired about the present number of Jews in the Holy Land and was told by Catholic monks that

"When the Jews were driven from Spain, many came to the Levant, but their numbers have been dreadfully thinned by the plague, of which 3,000 died only last year in the Holy Land."

1.

1. Mishkenot Shaananim. The quarter was the first to be built beyond the walls of the Old City of Jerusalem. It was begun with a donation from Judah Touro, a New Orleans Jew. The neighbourhood was built on the initiative of Sir Moses Montefiore; it was completed in 1860.
The Jews of Jerusalem were afraid to leave the safety of the walled Old City, and the settlement of the new quarter was accomplished only by the endeavour of the more courageous among the city's Jews.
To enable the inhabitants of the quarter to earn their livelihood, Montefiore built a flour-mill at the end of the quarter which is still extant.
Next to this quarter another residential project was established in 1894 called Yemin Moshe, after Sir Moses.

2. The "Hurva" synagogue. Rabbi Yehuda the Hassid (Judah the Pious) came to the Land of Israel in 1700 and settled in Jerusalem with his followers and pupils. He began to erect a house of worship, but a short time after his arrival he died and, with construction activity on the project halted, the half-finished building stood for many years like a ruin — whence the name: the Hurva ("ruin") of Rabbi Yehuda the Hassid. In 1857 construction was resumed, and in 1864 the synagogue was completed.

2.

About the town of Safad, he supplies the following information:

"(Safad) contains, they said, from 1,000 to 1,500 houses, of which from 300 to 350 are Jewish and the rest Turkish."
(W. Turner, *Journal of a Tour in the Levant*, Vol. 2, p. 1110–1113.)

T. R. Joliffe, an English traveller who visited the country in 1817, states:

"It is said that the number of people living in Tiberias is 4,000, of which two-thirds are Jews."

Two estimates of the number of Jews in the Land of Israel are given here. The earliest was made by W. T. Young, the first British Consul in Jerusalem. The second one was made by Rev. J. Nicolayson, an English missionary who lived in Jerusalem after 1833.

The Tiferet Israel Synagogue, better known as Nissan Bak, after the name of its founder, who was an active member of Jerusalem's Ashkenazic Jewish community. The building was dedicated in 1865 and was given the name Tiferet Israel, after the Rabbi of Rozin and Sadigora, Israel Friedman, who was the leading spirit behind its construction. In 1869, the Austrian Emperor Franz Josef visited Jerusalem, and it was he who contributed the cupola to the building, which was completed in 1871. Following the seizure of the Jewish Quarter in 1948, the building was demolished by the Jordanians.

1. A drawing of the holy places in the country, probably 19th century.

2. A section of an illustrated map of the country by Rabbi Shlomo Haim Pini, a resident of Safad. The drawing shows the town of Tiberias encircled by a wall and, outside the city, the graves of famous rabbinical scholars.

NUMBER OF JEWS IN THE LAND OF ISRAEL

	Young's Report	Nicolayson's Estimate
Jerusalem	5,000–6,000	6,000–7,000
Nablus	150– 200	200
Tiberias	600– 700	1,200
Safad	1,500–2,000	—
Haifa	150– 200	150– 200
Jaffa	60	60
Acre	200	—
Villages in Galilee	400– 580	400– 500

The two estimates given above were included in the report of A. A. Bonar and R. M. McCheyne, a pair of English missionaries sent to Palestine by the Church of Scotland in 1839 for the purpose of converting the Jews.

Felix Bovet, a Protestant theologian who visited the Land of Israel in 1858, asserted:

"The Christians who conquered the Land of Israel did not know how to hold it and it was never anything more to them than a battleground and a graveyard. The Saracens who took it from them also left and it was then taken by the Turks and the Ottomans who are still there. They have made a desert of it where it is scarcely possible to walk without fear. Even the Arabs who dwell there do so as temporary sojourners. They set their tents wherever there is pasture and seek refuge in the ruins of the towns. They did not create anything as they were in truth strangers, not masters of the Land. The spirit of the desert, which had brought them thither, could in the same fashion take them away again and leave nothing behind. God who has given Palestine to so many nations has not permitted any one to establish itself or to take root in it. No doubt it is reserved for his people Israel, for those rebellious children who one day will become the men of meek and humble spirit of whom Jesus said — They shall inherit the earth."

CONCLUSION

Until the 19th century, the traditionally religious type of community, such as those in the holy cities of Jerusalem, Safad, Tiberias, and Hebron, was predominant.

During the 19th century, immigration increased, as the English missionary, W.H. Bartlett, records in his book, *Jerusalem Revisited*, London 1855, that the Jewish community in Jerusalem numbered over 11,000. This is confirmed by the second British consul in Jerusalem, James Finn, in his book *Stirring Times*, London 1878. Mary Elisa Rogers writes in her book, *Domestic Life in Palestine*, London 1862, that there was an active Jewish community in Haifa. She lived there with her brother, the British vice-consul, from 1850 to 1859. The English missionary, Andrew Bonar, who visited the Holy Land in 1839, mentioned the synagogue of the Jews in Nablus besides that of the Samaritans (*Narrative of a Mission of Enquiry to the Jews . . .* Edinburgh 1846). The American officer W.F. Lynch who arrived in the country in 1848 describes the Jewish community in Jaffa in his *Narrative of the U.S.'s expedition to the River Jordan and the Dead Sea*, London 1852. All these communities were urban in nature and attempts by Jewish philanthropists abroad to establish rural villages had, so far, failed.

In 1870, the Mikveh Israel Agricultural School was founded near Jaffa. This was followed almost immediately by the establishment of villages in Motza (Jerusalem) and, in 1878, in Petah Tikvah.

The rise of nationalism in Europe and the Russian pogroms of the 1880's led to a new wave of immigration. The names given by these immigrants to the villages which they founded reflect the vision and ideals represented by them — Rishon LeZion (the First in Zion), Nes Ziona (the Banner of Zion), Yesud HaMa'ala (the Start of the Ascent) and Rosh Pina (Cornerstone). The deterioration in economic conditions in the Land of Israel adversely affected settlement and threatened the total collapse of agricultural enterprises. The Jews of the Diaspora and the Jewish philanthropists, particularly Baron Edmond de Rothschild, came to the rescue.

In 1904, the second great wave of immigration, known as the Second Aliyah, began. This, too, was ideologically motivated, being based on the principles of Jewish labour, independent agricultural settlement and the brotherhood and equality of men. Subsequently the revolutionary forms of settlement we know today — the kibbutz (collective settlement) and the moshav (cooperative small-holders' village) — were established. The Hebrew language, long relegated to liturgical or literary usage, was revived as a spoken tongue.

The World Zionist Organisation began to create the necessary tools for consolidating Jewish settlement, such as the Workers' Bank, the Jewish National Fund, whose task was to purchase land for the nation, and many other institutions dedicated to the mission of national revival.

The Balfour Declaration, issued by the British in 1917, recognising the right of the Jews to a national home in Palestine, and the subsequent Mandate for Palestine, in which the League of Nations incorporated this aim, served as the international recognition of what was to become the State of Israel in 1948.

It has been our purpose, and, we hope, a not unsuccessful one, to bring to the reader a factual and convincing testimony of a vibrant, diversified and safely-anchored continuity of Jewish presence and performance in the Land of Israel through millennia of alien conquest. We document a widespread and far-ranging presence and a manifold performance — in farm and workshop, in devout learning and encyclopaedic scholarship, and in the bearing of arms if bidden.

That loyal, tireless and dedicated Jewry, minuscule but always a magnet for brethren still exiled, brethren drawn homewards hopefully by its resolute example, was 'Watchman of the Shrine', guardian of the Jewish heritage, for century after century of Dispersion.

Thus was kept and strengthened the link between People and Land.

Index of References

Dio Cassius in *Dio's Roman History* with an English translation by E. Cary, Vol. VIII, Book LXIX (London, 1925).

St. Jerome (Hieronymus), *Hieronymi Chronicon*, ed. R. Helm (Berlin, 1913–1926).

St. Jerome (Hieronymus), Commentary to the Book of Zephaniah in J. P. Migne, *Patrologia Latina*, Vol. XXV (Paris, 1845).

Eusebius, *History of the Martyrs of Palestine*, edited and translated into English by W. Cureton (London, 1861).

Bar-Zoma, Chronicle published in *Revue de l'Orient Chrétien*, Vol. 19 (Paris, 1913–1914).

J. Malalas, *Chronographia* (Bonn, 1831).

Euthychius, *Histoire de Yahya ibn Sa'id d'Antioche* (Paris, 1924–1932).

Canonici Hebronensis Tractatus de inventione sanctorum patriarcharum Abraham, Ysaac et Jacob, *Recueil des Historiens des Croisades* (His. Occ.) (Paris, 1895).

Mujir ed-Din, *al-Uns al-Jalil, History of Jerusalem and Hebron* (Cairo, 1866–1867).

Muqaddasi, *Knowledge of Climes*, edited De Goeje (Leiden, 1906).

Kirkisani, *The Book of Lights and Watchtowers*, edited Leon Nemoy (New York, 1939–1940).

Nasir-i-Khusrau, *Book of Travels* (Teheran, 1917).

M. Ladoire, *Voyage fait à la Terre Sainte en l'année MLCCXIX* (Paris, 1720).

Albert of Aachen, *Chronicon Hierosolymitanum* (Helmstedt, 1584).

Dimashqi, *Knowledge of Wonders at Sea and on Land* (St. Petersburg, 1866).

Jacques of Verona, *Liber Peregrinationis* (Rome, 1950).

Ogier d'Anglure, *Le Saint Voyage de Jérusalem*, ed. F. Bonnardot et A. Longnon (Paris, 1878).

Pantaléao de Aveiro, *Itinerario da Terra Sancta*, ed. Antonio Baiao (Coimbra, 1927).

William Biddulph, *The Travels of Four Englishmen and a Preacher* (London, 1609).

P. Belon, *Les observations de plusieurs singularités et choses mémorables* (Paris, 1588).

Ignatius von Rheinfelden, *New Jerusalemite Pilgrimages* (Constance, 1664).

William Turner, *Journal of a Tour in the Levant* (London, 1820).

Letters and Documents discovered in the *Cairo Genizah*, published by J. Mann in *The Jews in Egypt and in Palestine under the Fatimid Caliphs* (New York, 1920).

Acknowledgements

We would like to thank the following people, publishing houses and institutions for allowing us to reproduce maps and photographs.

Prof. Yigael Yadin

Kindler (Museum Haaretz, Tel Aviv) — Illustrations from his *Coins in Eretz Israel* and *Among the Nations* (Hebrew)

"Am Oved" Publishers from their book by Ish Shalom *Christian Travellers in Palestine* (Hebrew)

The Department of Antiquities and Museums, Jerusalem

Kibbutz Meuchad Publishing Company for a photograph from *Research in Our Land* (Hebrew) by I. Barslavi

Mossad Harav Kook for photographs from *Synagogues in Eretz Israel* by Fincarfeld (Hebrew) and *Holy Tombstones in Eretz Israel* by Zev Vilnay

Israel Exploration Society, Jerusalem, for photographs from *Encyclopedia of Excavations*

Gazith Publishing for extracts from their art and literary journal

Massada Publishing Company for photographs from *Jewish Art* by Ruth Efron

Mossad Bialik — *Sefer Hayishuv* and *Encyclopaedia Biblica*

Oxford University Press for permission to reproduce the following:

> *Khirbet el Mefjer* by R. W. Hamilton — Plate XCIV:2
> *Ottoman Documents* by U. Heyd — photograph of Document No. 11

Père Bénoit, Ecole Biblique et Archéologique Française, Jerusalem, from *Les Grottes de Muraba'at* — Plate XLVI:43, Plate XXII:4

Israel Museum, Jerusalem

Hebrew Union College, Cincinnati

Department of Archaeology, Hebrew University of Jerusalem

The Jewish National and University Library

Palphot Ltd. Herzlia, for use of colour slides

Photographs — Micha Pen, Jerusalem
              David Harris, Jerusalem

Max Nurock

Many other scholars advised us on the publication. It would be difficult to acknowledge each one individually and we are sincerely grateful to all who assisted and contributed.

First Edition   October 1975
Second Edition   August 1976
Jerusalem
©
Produced and Published by
The Israel Economist
P.O.B. 7052, Jerusalem
Tel. 234131-2-3

Composer typesetting and graphics
at The Israel Economist Studio

Printed by: GACI
Graphic Arts Committee for Israel (U.S.A.)